For Kim, from Sheila. July 7th 1946.

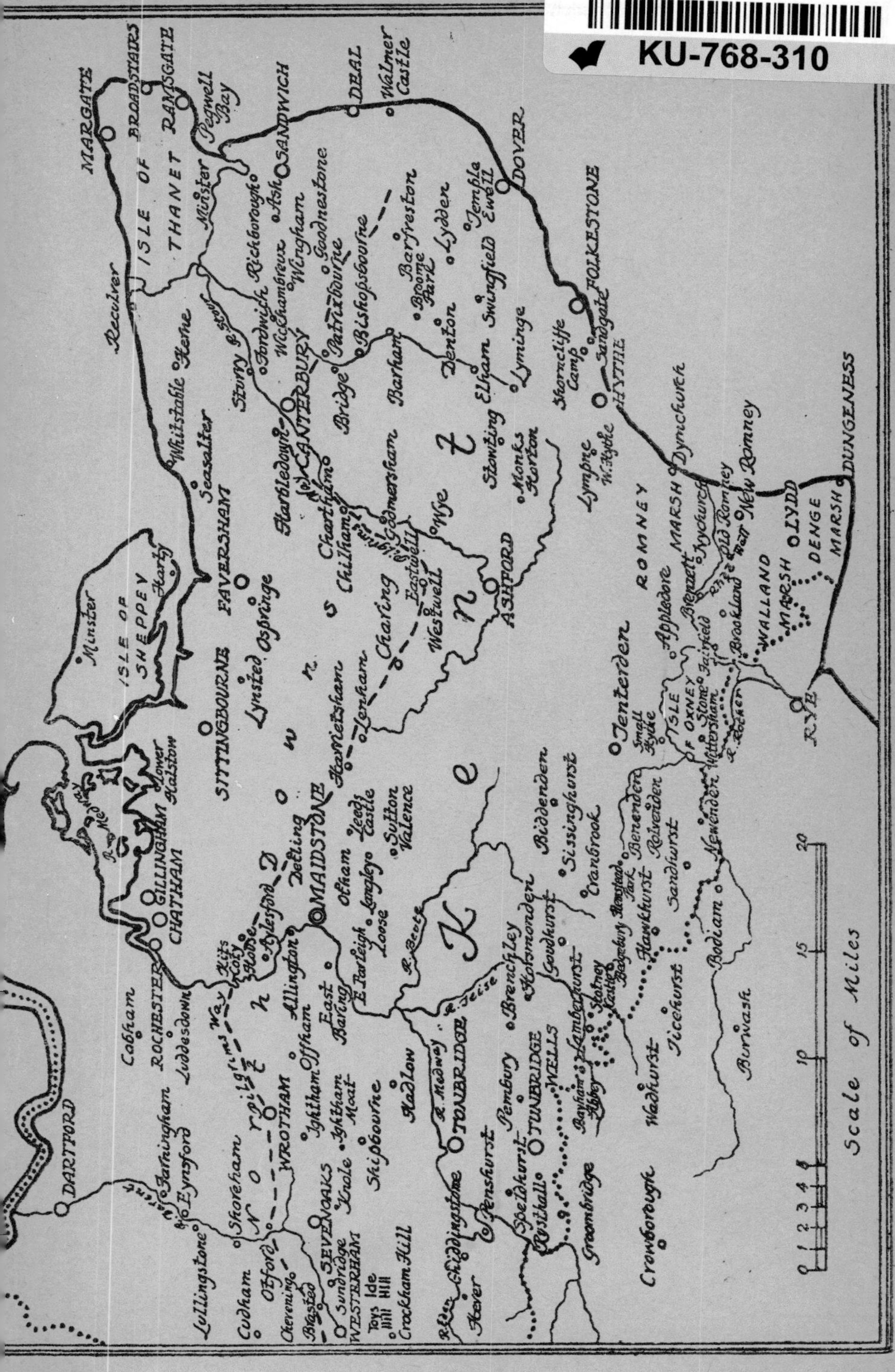

THE HOME COUNTIES

The Face of Britain

Uniform Volumes in the Series

SHAKESPEARE'S COUNTRY
By JOHN RUSSELL
(10/6 *net*)

ENGLISH LAKELAND
By DOREEN WALLACE

COTSWOLD COUNTRY
By H. J. MASSINGHAM

CHILTERN COUNTRY
By H. J. MASSINGHAM

EAST ANGLIA
By DOREEN WALLACE

ENGLISH DOWNLAND
By H. J. MASSINGHAM

SOUTH-EASTERN SURVEY
By RICHARD WYNDHAM

WEST COUNTRY
By C. HENRY WARREN

NORTH COUNTRY
By EDMUND VALE

THE HIGHLANDS OF
SCOTLAND
By HUGH QUIGLEY

THE LOWLANDS OF
SCOTLAND
By GEORGE SCOTT-MONCRIEFF

THE FACE OF IRELAND
By MICHAEL FLOYD

WELSH BORDER COUNTRY
By P. T. JONES

B. T. BATSFORD LTD.
15 NORTH AUDLEY STREET, LONDON, W.1
and MALVERN WELLS, WORCESTERSHIRE

From a Watercolour by Myles Birket Foster, R.W.S.

A SURREY LANE

THE FACE OF BRITAIN

The
HOME COUNTIES

MIDDLESEX, SURREY, KENT,
HERTFORDSHIRE AND ESSEX

By

S. P. B. MAIS

*Illustrated from Photographs
and Drawings*

LONDON
B. T. BATSFORD LTD
15 NORTH AUDLEY STREET, W.1
& MALVERN WELLS, WORCESTERSHIRE

A SELECTION OF THE AUTHOR'S
MANY OTHER BOOKS:—

HILLS OF THE SOUTH
ATLANTIC COAST EXPRESS
BLACK SPIDER
THERE'LL ALWAYS BE AN ENGLAND
THIS UNKNOWN ISLAND
SEE ENGLAND FIRST
ROUND ABOUT ENGLAND
PICTORIAL BRITAIN
LISTEN TO COUNTRY
ISLES OF THE ISLAND
HIGHWAYS AND BYWAYS IN THE WELSH MARCHES
BRITAIN CALLING
ALL DAYS OF MY LIFE
ETC., ETC.

FIRST PUBLISHED WINTER 1942–3

BOOK
PRODUCTION
WAR ECONOMY
STANDARD

*This book is produced in
complete conformity with the
authorized economy standard*

MADE AND PRINTED IN GREAT BRITAIN
FOR THE PUBLISHERS, B. T. BATSFORD LTD., LONDON
BY UNWIN BROTHERS LTD., WOKING

PREFATORY NOTE

NEVER before in our long history has the word "home" meant so much to us.

It is not only those men in the fighting forces far afield who are battling to preserve the security of home who think longingly of it, but also those many hundreds of thousands who are temporarily banished from the counties that to them mean home. Probably nine-tenths of the nation are suffering from a nostalgia that is seldom absent from the mind even in sleep.

After the war what a tremendous home-coming there will be, what rich compensations for our present deprivations.

In the meantime to buoy us up for the struggle it is good to conjure up visions of the woods and downs, the heaths and commons, little rivers and village greens of the counties that we know as home.

S. P. B. M.

ACKNOWLEDGMENT

THE Publishers desire to express their indebtedness to the following photographers, whose work is included in the illustrations: the late Brian C. Clayton, for Figs. 8, 44, 45, 46, 48, 49, 50, 51; Howard H. Camburn, Tunbridge Wells, Fig. 37; H. Bedford Lemere, Fig. 19; Dorien Leigh, Ltd., Figs. 2, 18, 30, 31, 34, 41, 43, 52, 54, 55, 56, 57, 69, 71, 77, 80, 93, 95; E. O. Hoppé, Figs. 2. 30, 31, 43, 55, 56, 80, 93, 95; the Mustograph Agency, Figs. 3, 5, 9, 11, 12, 25, 26, 28, 38, 42, 47, 53, 73, 74, 76, 81, 82, 83, 84, 85, 86, 87, 88, 91, 92, 94, 97, 98, 99; John H. Stone, Malvern, Figs. 13, 65, 66, 70; the late Rev. F. Sumner, Fig. 21; Will F. Taylor, Reigate, 7, 14, 15, 16, 17, 22, 23, 24, 27, 29, 32, 35, 39, 58, 59, 60, 67, 68, 72, 75, 90, 96; Verrall's Photo Service, 4, 33; Major R. Wyndham, 6, 20, 36, 40.

The provenance of the drawings is as follows: (the numbers are those of the pages on which the illustrations occur) the late F. Chancellor, by kind permission of F. Wykeham Chancellor, F.R.I.B.A., 119; the late F. L. B. Griggs, R.A., by kind permission of Messrs. Macmillan and Co. Ltd., 111; the late J. Alfred Gotch, 48; W. Curtis Green, R.A., 10 (after the late L. A. Shuffrey), 35; Sydney R. Jones, 25, 32, 41, 52, 56; the late Roland W. Paul, 78 (by kind arrangement of *The Builder*), 81; M. and C. H. B. Quennell, 17, 121; the remainder are from the Publishers' Collection.

Of the colour plates, Figs. 10 and 64 are from the collections of the Victoria and Albert Museum, South Kensington, and are included by kind permission of the Director.

CONTENTS

ERRATUM

Plate 10.—*For Artist's name* JOHN SCORER *read* JOHN GLOVER

2   THE ENTRANCE, IGHTHAM MOTE, KENT

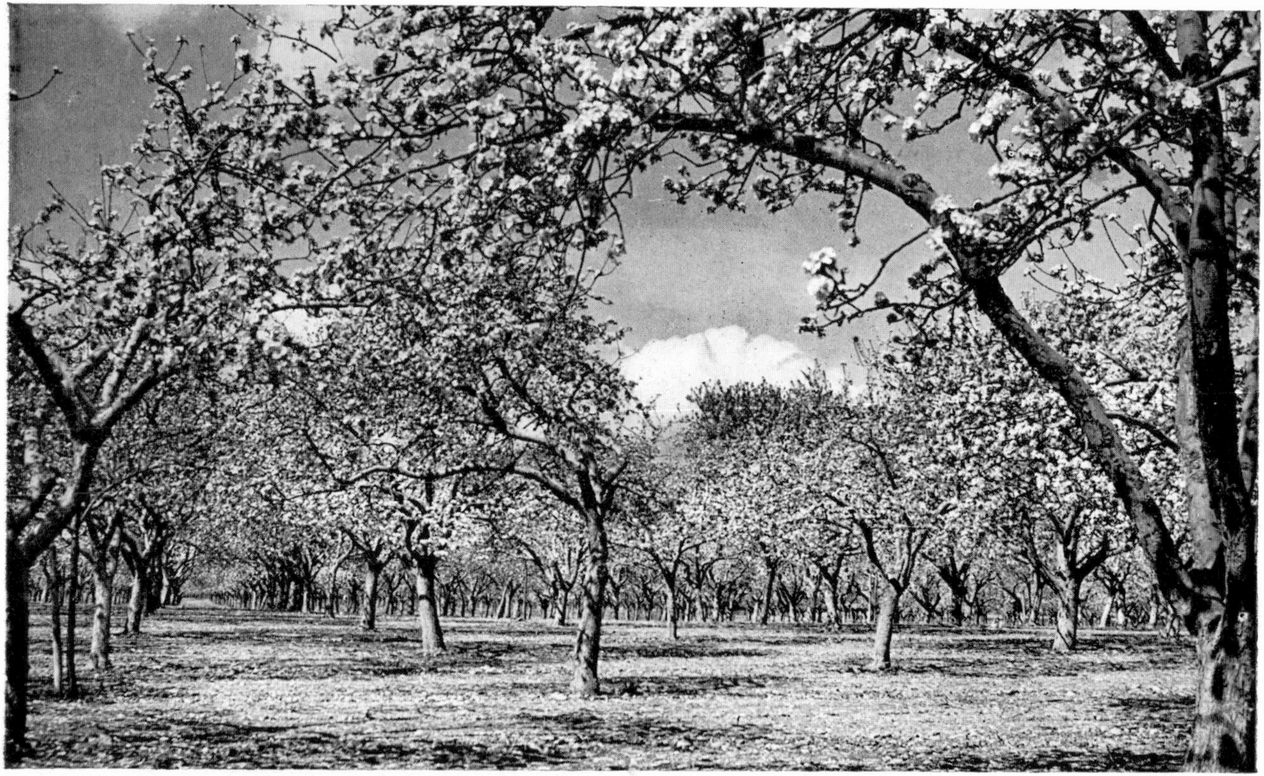

3 A KENTISH APPLE-ORCHARD IN FLOWER, NEAR MAIDSTONE

INTRODUCTION

THE phrase "Home Counties" may give but a vague impression to many, like that still more mysterious expression "The Shires"; for our present purpose we shall regard the area as comprising the five counties around London County—Middlesex, Hertfordshire, Essex, Kent and Surrey. Strictly speaking, Hertfordshire is always separated from the town by a piece of Middlesex, but it comes largely into the London postal and police districts; for reasons of space the temptation to include Berkshire, Sussex and with a few single exceptions, Buckinghamshire has been firmly resisted. The most arbitrary divorce is the excision of Sussex from its two other south-eastern cousins; by this we cut off the South Downs from the North, though we get in most of the Weald. And indeed the area covered is ample enough to satisfy anyone, and to stay outside the province of any one person to know *au fond*; it is for the critical to point out that it is a pity that we have not managed a more adequate treatment of our district, or made better use of our opportunities.

The Home Counties have been brought by this war to a vital factor in the lives of thousands who would otherwise perhaps have never known the parts into which they have been thrust. It will be all to the good if they can realise something of the interest and attraction of their war-time environment. Offices, factories, banks, warehouses have moved outward to varying distances; schools have settled in all sorts of country houses; hospitals and other institutions have gone some way afield, and thousands of ordinary folk have swelled the mounting populations of country districts, those of them, that is, who could squeeze their way in, thus intensifying and accentuating a movement which has been gathering strength for the last few decades. The Home Counties are fully playing their part in the war; as a natural consequence they are playing a greater part in the lives of myriads of English folk, be it for the time or for good and all.

This area, or much of its inner extent, is labelled by geographers The London Basin; writers of brochures often refer to it as London's Country. It is as though it were imagined, involuntarily perhaps, that these counties had not enough to stand on for their own account, but were conceived as adjuncts to the capital. We refuse to acknowledge the supremacy of the Metropolis; let us try to earn the approval of the shade of Cobbett by ignoring the Wen, keeping rather towards the top edge of the Basin or staying the hither side of its rim. Hence we have not prescribed any routes radiating outward from inner or even outer London, as has so often been worked out; let us rather wander here and there over this quintet of unassuming English counties. Indeed they will admirably repay odd rambling, for at their best they abound in winding, deep-hedged lanes, quiet casual hamlets, heaths and commons, and paths by the brookside. Till this tyranny be over-past we are all bound to restrict the extent of our country wanderings, but that does not mean we should abandon them,—we none of us know, understand or appreciate enough the quiet beauty of our nearer landscapes, the appeal of sterling building, material expressions of that form of life for which we are glad to fight and strive. We shall battle and work all the more fiercely if our scanty leisure has brought us into closer contact with nature in the open country, to the improvement of our health and the healing of our spirits. There is nothing unpatriotic in seeing our own nearer counties within reasonable limits, and no regulation comes between the Englishman and his own countryside, though some of the austerity-for-its-own-sake brigade would pin us to our own back-gardens. No one would wish to waste petrol or coal, but there is shanks' pony and the cycle, which with a little local public-vehicular assistance can carry us to remunerative places. This war has meant a return to comparative immobility, season-ruled diet and all sorts of primitiveness; among these may be reckoned the possibility of some slight hostility to strangers on the part of rural dwellers. If they withhold information, the initiated are not usually dependent on casual tips and have their own reference material. If they put the police on you, there is usually no difficulty in reassuring the village bobby, who is rarely devoid of friendly common-sense. It is for those who drop from the skies that real wrath is reserved; the unfortunate crew of a forced-landed British bomber returning from France were received with grim and chilling suspicion by the local Home Guard, and with curses and flints by the deadlier females.

This method of covering a selected district by a number of suggested routes is convenient, but has its emphatic drawbacks and must be reckoned as by no means ideal. I am quite prepared to admit that this plan of quartering a batch of counties by selected rambles is, to borrow Beethoven's expression on Resignation, a miserable expedient, *ein elendes Hülfsmittel*, but God help me I can do no other. I should have liked to have produced a work in which the country was classified according to types: the Thames Estuary, the Chalk, Woods and Heaths, etc., with chapters on old Houses, Villages, Literary Associations, Suburbanisation, etc. I got as far as producing a syllabus which pleased me, but could not translate it into words. In fact this had to be regretfully abandoned as impracticable at present; war work and conditions do not permit of the necessary research, and an amount of exploration is required for such comparative analysis which is out of the question today. But perhaps something of the kind can be essayed after the war, if the public would like to have it.

There are doubtless some people who regard the idea of any
book on the Home Counties (actually there have not been very
many) as unnecessary, indeed absurd. "The man is daft", I hear
them saying, "to think of an account of counties that have been
overrun and suburbanised, and now serve very largely as metropolitan dormitories or advance posts." I have heard the same
argument advanced in regard to the Chilterns, in which it is far
from being the fact, and it is still less true when applied to these
five counties, which contain many quiet countrified areas, fine
views, extensive forests, remote hamlets, rural villages, distinctive
cottages and farms, historic country houses and unspoilt churches
both great and small. It is impossible to do more than to submit
a few typical specimens to serve as fingerposts or possibly as
reminders.

These counties can offer us a remarkable variety in unity; both
in the country itself and in man's contribution which he has laid
on it in the shape of buildings.

It is a matter for discussion whether they can hold their own
with the areas surrounding Oxford, Bristol or Birmingham; certainly there is little to choose between in that quartet, and it is
usually a matter of individual taste or preference. Now our counties
of course belong throughout to the newer geological formations of
softer stuff, which explains why building stone can only be found
in one or two isolated spots, but gives them the suave and genial
types of landscapes which may be regarded as typically Southern
English. The heights we can show are all caused by the chalk and
the sand; from the central boss in the Wiltshire chalk the white
hills north of the Thames sweep in a broad band north-east to the
top part of Essex; to the south the long arm of the North Downs
sweeps in a verdant flattened arc to the east and swings southward
to Dover. The sandy Forest Ridge spreads from South-West
Surrey, and then clings patchily close to the southern edge of the
chalk with only the narrow Holmesdale valley between till it dies
away. There is also further south a hilly, sandy, wooded section
round Tunbridge Wells which wanders on eastward with diminishing undulations, after filling North-East Sussex with the heaths
of Ashdown Forest. The absence of this sandy area is the outstanding difference between the two sides of the Thames; apart
from the chalk Hertfordshire and Essex consist largely of undulating farmlands. The coastal flats, marshes and estuaries of Essex
are matched by the north shore of Kent; e.g. the Isle of Grain, the
Isle of Sheppey and around; in fact but for the cliffs of Dover
there is little that is striking about this south-east coastline, though
its creeks make it in peace time a happy hunting-ground of the
cruising yachtsman. The great expanse of Romney Marsh, on the
other hand (39, 40), is a very individual district with the attraction
of great expanses and enormous skyscapes. "The green cattle-
dotted plain, with its gleaming water-lines, is not without beauty

when overlooked from the adjoining heights,—often presenting singular effects of light." But after all it is the "plain-pudding", hedge chequerwork, undulating farm country that predominates in most parts, and this is as it should be, for such landscapes are typical, and nearer and dearer to us than ever as we realise that it is the farmers' patient unremitting skill that stands between us and the submarine-induced starvation which the fascist dictators so ardently desire for us. Once again let us hope that man will speak, not in this time of crisis but hereafter, of the "tall Essex wheat", and that we shall agree with Charles Lamb that Hertford-shire is "that fine corn country"(84).

Among the infinity of wide views which even the modest heights of the Home Counties can afford there are the stretches of the clay plain from the Chilterns and their north-eastern continua-tion, e.g. Ivinghoe Beacon, Therfield or Heydon, and the im-mense southward views of the Weald from the Leith Hill trio (14, 23), Reigate Hill and many North Down vantage-spots, and Ide Hill and its fellows, Toys Hill and Crockham Hill, farther east. Essex can also show its wide prospects from Danbury, the Warleys or Laindon Hill. There is plenty of woodland apart from the Corporation of London's Epping Forest and Burnham Beeches —the Chilterns are densely wooded with beech, though further north they turn to bare and rolling downs,—and there are the remains of the old Enfield Chase, not far from Hertford. In Surrey and less in Kent the chalk has often thick lonely woods, and the sandy heights from Hindhead to Maidstone have their own covering of pine, bracken, scrub-oak and gorse. But some may prefer the hazel copses or oakwoods round the "Folds" or even like best the numberless little copses scattered over the face of the land. In spring they are dotted with primrose clumps and starred with wild anemones, and later carpeted with sheets of bluebells. In autumn the beeches glow yellow to scarlet and the oaks keep their russet tones well into November. In the depths of midwinter the heath country that some find repellent in the leafy months stands out in its mantle of dark green flecked with the brown of the young scrub trees. There are river valleys enough to explore; if some of the larger streams have been canalised or industrialised, we can follow the Mole (57), the Wey (17, 59), the Eden and parts of the Medway (7), and the eastern Rother with a host of smaller brooks and streams.

North and south alike abound in narrow byways and winding lanes in which I for one feel restfully at home; they are cut deep into soft sandstone with the green boughs meeting overhead; they drop steeply to the white weatherboarded mill with its reedy wind-ruffled pool, or ever twist past the group of tile-hung cottages or gabled timber farmhouses set back behind demure palings.

There is not so much occasion for lachrymose jeremiads on the question of suburbanisation—the tendency for city workers to live further out is a healthy one, and we can be glad that they can sleep within sight of green fields; fortunately the country nearest the towns is not usually outstanding; certainly there has been an amazing growth since the first Great War, to think only of the vast settlements around Alperton, Queensbury, South Harrow, Romford, Ruislip, Worcester Park, Kenton and the once lonely little hamlet of Preston, the home of John Lyon, the founder of Harrow School. It is worse when a nice little old market town is disfigured into amorphous urbanism, such as perhaps Hemel Hempstead, or a pleasant village is "developed" into the unattractive incoherence of Pembury. Government departments show a perverse malignity in appropriating the best scenery for purposes which could equally well be carried out elsewhere, and county councils, frequently as lacking in public spirit as they are devoid of taste, may often be counted on to do the wrong thing. Nevertheless the steadily mounting list of scenic splendours and fine buildings in the safe hands of the National Trust is a cause for thankful encouragement, and the idea of the Green Belt is one of noble and far-sighted vision. The day is far removed from the execrable impost of "undeveloped land duty"in the Lloyd George "Gospel" budget of 1909. Any proposal that an owner should be tax-penalised for keeping his fields out of the maw of the speculative builder would cause its perpetrator to be mobbed in the House and flayed in the press. A friend of mine bought a house at Hendon and was asked to pay 13s. 2d. undeveloped land duty; the land had been actually developed and he was wild at being told that it was "deemed" to be unbuilt on and he was "deemed" (a favourite affectation of officialdom to found administration and extortion on the thing which is *not*) to be the landowner when he paid ground rent. In a protracted acrimonious skirmish he finally insisted on a detailed analysis of how the varying demand-figures were arrived at, and Somerset House abandoned the struggle. He rejoiced greatly when in the annual report the Inland Revenue complained plantively of the exceeding great difficulty of collecting this detestable duty, now happily defunct.

Heaven be thanked there are more delightful old market towns in the Home Counties than I can find space to mention, and many of them are quite locally distinctive—Saffron Walden (90), Maldon (95), Baldock, Buntingford, Farnham (18), Guildford, Cranbrook, Tenterden, Westerham have many fellows apart from Canterbury or Maidstone. There are quite a number which leave me guessing as to whether they are villages or towns; if you make a shot you are sure to offend the people, and to call them village-towns does not solve the question. While as for the villages, they are as numerous as their attractiveness is diversified. Mr. Pakington gives Finchingfield, which some malign influence is trying to spoil, West Wycombe which I have strayed to visit, Chilham and Westmill in his two "teams" of fifteen stars. But in addition there are high up Eynsford, Otford, Ightham (53) and Havering atte Bower, and Denham almost within the metropolitan orbit, and of course plenty more scattered around. There are villages round wide greens like Shamley Green, Aldbury, Chiddingfold and Groombridge, and Offham with its quintain, long street villages such as Biddenden (p. 41) and many another, riverside villages, scattered group places like Ashwell (80), and star-clusters of delightful hamlets such as the "fields" of the Pant Valley and the "folds" of the Surrey–Sussex border. Then we recall the Steventon-Hendred-Hagbourne string, just outside our reach, and of course the Kentish "dens"; do not let us forget the hill-top group which is smaller but precious, e.g. Looseley Row, Goudhurst, and of course Brill, which I must stray to mention, for if it is really in Bucks it is only a few miles from the Hertfordshire north-west border, and from the edge of the South-West Chilterns which we shall explore together in Chapter XVI. I would like to hurry away and do homage to them all.

As for country houses, our area is as rich as any part of England, from the smallest manorhouse to the stateliest palace. It is safe to say that no period from the earliest to the end of the Regency is unrepresented in these counties, and such places as Knole (54–6), Penshurst (27) and Hever are as remarkable for their treasures of craftsmanship as for their great historical associations. It is impossible to mention more than a few in detail: let us be content that there are Norman castle keeps, quiet smaller mediaeval dwellings, Tudor manorhouses, Elizabethan halls great and small, examples of the transition from early to late Renaissance, medium sized houses of late Stuart symmetry, Palladian mansions, Adam houses, and work of Regency stucco. The domestic contribution of Hertfordshire and Essex *inter alia* is recorded in the painstaking volumes of the Historical Monuments Commission, four volumes being assigned to the latter county. It is lamentable, however, that they stopped short arbitrarily with the death of Queen Anne in 1712. A remarkably interesting volume by Mr. Oswald has been devoted to the houses of Kent, and who shall say that they are not worth it? There is no phase or style of English house design which is not worthily represented in that extremely rich county's area of excellent domestic building.

Many of these houses are open to the public, in normal times at least, regularly or occasionally; in addition a number of fine gardens are accessible on stated days for a small fee in aid of the local nursing association, and this practice is continued in part at least in war time. I had thought of making a chronological table of the houses specially worthy of note in the five counties; it would be great fun to do even in a brief form, but the times are too unsettled for it to be of much practical service.

I have drifted from towns and villages to houses, but should perhaps have made earlier mention of the churches, which are by no means so outstanding as the domestic work; they include nevertheless a number of fine and interesting fabrics. Essex in its church architecture stands apart from the two counties of the old kingdom of East Anglia, which were far more industrialised by the mediaeval wool trade. Nevertheless the standard of the county craftsmanship is high and the use of less usual materials skilful and enterprising. The builders were undaunted by the absence of

WEST HANNINGFIELD BELFRY   FRYERNING TOWER

ESSEX TIMBER AND BRICK

building stone; they developed a finished technique in brick, often diapered with patterns in dark purple, in which towers, clerestories, etc., are all effectively and ably worked out with such details as battlements, parapets, and similar features. There is space to mention only such few instances as Sandon, Fryerning (above), Castle Hedingham, Woodham Walter, Great Baddow and Ingrave. In some instances, as at Layer Marney the arcade itself is of brick; a few arcades such as Shenfield are entirely of timber, with more examples in which there is a wooden arch or two. But it is the timber belfries that make up the most individual Essex contribution to ecclesiology—supported on vast baulks of massive timber they rise in slender pyramids or blunt, sometimes in diminishing stages as at Blackmore; at West Hanningfield from the plan of a Greek cross (pp. 7, 132). Margaretting may be instanced as typical (92); it bears a cousinly resemblance to High Halden across the Thames. Naturally there is a wide, indeed, practically complete, range in size and elaboration from humble little primitive structures with their wooden bellcotes (88) such as you find, say, among the Easters, Lavers and Rodings and some Norman apsidal primitives as Little Braxted (p. 13), through noble spacious medium-sized buildings such as Castle Hedingham, High Easter or Dedham, to the splendour of such glorious fabrics as Thaxted (87); there is a similar range in time from the Saxon log nave of Greenstead-juxta-Ongar to the late Perpendicular of Saffron Walden.

Naturally the churches of Middlesex and Surrey have been most materially and largely affected by Metropolitan development and extension; in poor little Middlesex such small unassuming structures as Ickenham, old Kingsbury and Perivale with its weatherboarded tower remain to testify to the once rural character of the hamlets they serve. Then there is quite a group of mediaeval churches with good stone towers: Chiswick, Ruislip, spired Harrow and others. If Hendon has been enlarged out of its country character for a vast growth of population, South Mimms is still a village building of character, and Harefield, touched up about 1820, is remarkable for its rich openwork carved communion rails and the great series of Newdigate monuments. Then there is the Renaissance series with their craftsmanship; we can only think of Twickenham, Shepperton, Laleham and Whitchurch by Stanmore. Lastly there are a few scraggy fabrics of the early nineteenth century such as Hampton, Mill Hill, etc.

Surrey has naturally suffered painfully from rebuilding and the villainy of restoration; even buildings in early revival Gothick have not escaped, but the county can still show some characteristic indigenous churches; we can only mention St. Mary's Guildford, with Saxon tower and apse paintings (p. 18). Chipstead with its austere central tower, the timber belfries of Thursley and Crowhurst (25), large mixed buildings like Reigate and Farnham and such typical productions with shingled spires as Shere and Merstham (p. 70) and Great Bookham, for which we may be thankful. There are the early brasses of Stoke d'Abernon, the fine Ladder of Heaven mural at Chaldon, and the double chancel and Norman balustrade at Compton (21). The pro-Cathedral of Holy Trinity, Guildford, is a dignified Renaissance design.

We cannot do better than endorse the dictum of the faithful Murray that "the churches of Hertfordshire are extremely interesting, many of them being of considerable size and beauty and rich in monuments and brasses." Their little spirelets, "the Hertfordshire needle", are frequently found and form, in whatever

4   THE WESTERLY VIEW FROM THE CHURCH TOWER, GOUDHURST, KENT

material they occur, an engaging feature. Apart from St. Albans
Cathedral, Hemel Hempstead is fine Romanesque cruciform and
at the other end of the scale St. Leonard's Bengeo a little early
aisleless apsidal design; Sarratt is transeptal with saddle-back roof
tower. Among fine spacious town or large village fabrics are
Ashwell (80), Baldock, Hitchin, Anstey (79), and Bishop's Stortford. Kimpton, Aldenham and North Mimms (p. 75) are attractive
village churches, the latter pair unaffected by their proximity to
London, and Ayot St. Lawrence (p. 111) and St. Paul's Walden
chancel make a Late Renaissance contribution. The county is rich
in screens, as at Aldenham, Baldock, Kimpton, Hitchin and
Sandridge, with St. Albans chantries, and for post-Reformation
screen-work, Hatfield and St. Paul's Walden.

The churches of Kent are a mixed bag, and yet their typical
three-gable equal-width nave and aisles without clerestory is as
distinctive as in Cornwall, the other promontory right across
southern England. There is a county variety of Decorated tracery
as in the cathedral and Chartham chancel. There are all sorts of
towers—stumpy, austere, wide, squat, pyramid-roofed, but the
most typical are short and crowned by a shingled spire of timber-
broach type (41), or a tall ragstone tower with a prominent stair
turret projecting higher and itself battlemented; mention may be
made of Rodmersham, Cranbrook, Charing, Egerton, Lamberhurst (32), which with Rolvenden and Wittersham are good
examples. The "three-gable" arrangement is well seen at New
Romney, Lynsted, Westerham and Great Chart. Norman work is
represented at St. Margaret at Cliffe and in the rich elaboration of
Patrixbourne (45) and Barfreston (46, 50).

Fortunately all these counties can show a range of craftsmanship
in stone, wood , metal, painting and glass which will repay exploration in whatever district you happen to be situated. Richest of all
is the unending array of mediaeval and Renaissance monuments; it
is all to the good that we are at last beginning to realise something
of the glory of the heritage of post-Reformation tomb carving and
sculpture, and the day has gone for ever when it could be brushed
aside as "debased".

It is noteworthy that all the counties are united in producing
each in its own way a fine type of vernacular farmhouse and
cottage; Essex is well-known for its thatched plaster concealing
some sterling timber, in such places as the "fields" or Elmdon (82),
Wendens Ambo, etc., and in the coastal districts for black weather-
boarding which is general among farm buildings as in the Roding
country. Hertfordshire would seem less outstanding but that the
grand record of 400 drawings by J. C. Buckler of a century ago
(78, 79), exhibited in peace-time in the St. Alban's clock-tower
museum, shows what it possessed of splendid large half-timber
farmhouses, many of which are now lost to us. There are survivals,
often plastered, at Whitwell, Barkway, etc.

C

Our two southern counties are remarkable for their vernacular village buildings, which it has been suggested are the survivals of industrial development—in Kent the wool working trade, in Surrey possibly a group of minor industries. A volume has been devoted to the minor domestic work of the three south-eastern counties, but Surrey has had two entirely to itself, Ralph Nevill,

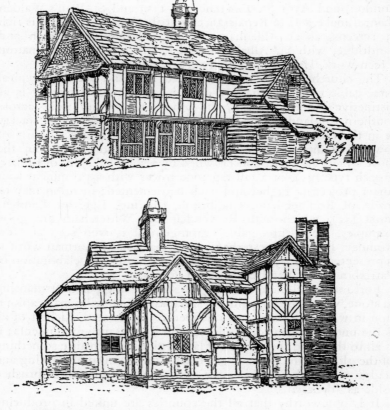

SURREY VERNACULAR: SUMMERSBURY FARM HOUSE, SURREY
IN 1874, BEFORE ALTERATION
Drawn by W. Curtis Green, R.A., from sketches by L. A. Shuffrey

1891, Curtis Green, 1908, but none of the three can be said to be exhaustive. The cottages are remarkable for their sense of texture; the half-timbering, plaster, brick, tile-hanging, weather-boarding, are all ample; sometimes several will occur on the same building with excellent effect. Apart from this, Surrey can show two star clusters of great farmhouses around Ockley and Shamley Green and many others elsewhere (19 and above). In Kent the most striking

6   THE CHURCH AND THE LAKE, EASTWELL PARK, KENT

7   THE BRIDGE OVER THE MEDWAY, EAST FARLEIGH, KENT

9 THE NORMAN LEAD FONT, WITH PANELS OF FIELD-
WORK, BROOKLAND, KENT

8 EARLY IRONWORK ON A CHURCH DOOR, THE
HORMEADS, HERTFORDSHIRE

production is the yeoman's house, with projecting side wings under one roof, originally central-halled. Apart from dwellings which shade into the country house we might select Stonehill, Chiddingly; Pattenden, Goudhurst (37), and examples at Shorne, near Sandwich, and elsewhere.

So much for the buildings of the Home Counties. On the human side, on which we cannot even briefly touch, there is a close ramifying network of historical associations which it is remunerative for everyone to trace, in part that is. There are battles, royal marriages, uprisings, murders, pilgrimages, landings, tribal gatherings, executions, martyrings and many another piece of the tragi-comic patterning of human life.

We can get much profit and gladness by touching lightly on the literary associations of the area, on which indeed quite an interesting book could be written, if sufficient people would take it to make it practicable to publish. For a few isolated instances, let us recall that the scene of the story of Swift and Stella is first laid among the quiet parklands of Waverley Abbey near Farnham; Jane Austen was happy in her sojourns in two other parks, Godmersham and Goodnestone in Kent, even if haunted by the ever present bane of servant tipping. The writings of Lamb are inte nsely interwoven with Hertfordshire, which gave rise to some of his most exquisite prose. As for St. Albans, Bacon of course lived at Gorhambury and lies in St. Michael's, and in College Street Cowper recovered from mental darkness under the kindly care of Dr. Cotton. He was born at Berkhamsted and endured dreadful bullying at Markyate Street School;—the poet was unfortunate in his Hertfordshire associations. Sir Philip Sidney is of course of Penshurst, and to make an incongruous coupling, Bulwer Lytton of Knebworth. There is perhaps some little excuse for working on Routes if we advance the plea that Chaucer's Pilgrimage is our first forerunner, though even he followed *longo intervallo* a main prehistoric trade route to the Continent. We shall meet the poet with his assorted company naturally on the Canterbury track, but almost anywhere we shall come across the sturdy figure of William Cobbett. Nearly five centuries part this tough old great-heart from the Frenchified Geoffrey, but both loved nature in their own way and have doubtless rejoiced together in their affection for England on the other side. We are bound to run across old Cobbett in Surrey, jogging his way along to or from the accursed Wen and, I make no doubt, in the other four of the Home Counties too, noting with approving satisfaction the neatness of careful farming, the excellence of trim and well-tended cottages, cursing angrily the arid desolation of barren heaths round Hindhead, and as we shall see, roused to frenzied eloquence of denunciation by the Tillingbourne at the iniquity of gunpowder and banknotes. John Evelyn is also to be remembered in Surrey, but as there is no greater contrast than between the meditative, introspective courtier

diarist and the fiery radical reformer, so the one was connected
almost entirely with his family place at Wotton, while the other
ranged far and wide. Yet both were alike in affectionate attach-
ment to the English countryside, and in their desire for its well-
being and improvement; the Restoration courtier advocated and
practised afforestation and silviculture; the Regency reformer was
instant in his desire for fine farming and a contented peasantry.

There is an unending range of subjects and features of varied
appeal if we have enough insight to discover and keenness to
record them. Whatever the closeness of the mesh of the sieves of
research and survey, there are unfailingly gleanings which we can
gather up, that nothing be lost or forgotten. Mr. G. T. Hine has
shown how sterling and valuable can be the contribution of a
local survey, in the immense number of historical facts he has
garnered and ordered on his native town of Hitchin and its
natural history. It is possible to make "collections" of such
pleasant byway subjects as dovecotes, village lockups, lychgates,
old bridges, farm buildings, graffiti on church walls, almshouses,
or inn-signs or even stiles. Place-names are perennially interest
ing,—Mr. H. M. Alderman in his *Pilgrimage in Hertfordshire**
lists over forty curiously-named hamlets, among which are Catlip,
Cupid Green, Heavensgate, Nasty, Pepperstock, Pigeons Wick,
Puddephats, Smug Oak, Sunnyside and Ugley. He has also
brought together an amusing collection of inn names, a subject
which makes a particular appeal to me; including with a number
of others such treasures as *The Old Guinea* (Ridge), *The Long Arm
& Short Arm* (Lemsford), *Old English Gentleman* (Cheshunt), *The
Cold Bath* (Hertford, opposite a Baptist Chapel), *Help-me-thro'-the-
World* (Codicote), *The Merry Month of May* (Bushey), *The Tom-in-
Bedlam* (Redbourne), *The Hermit of Redcoats* (Titmore Green),
The Chalk Drawers Arms (Colney Heath).

Geography like all vital things does make a difference,—whence
it comes that the Home Counties and especially the Kentish bulge
and the Thames Estuary have borne and must bear the most
frequent and heaviest aerial assaults of the Hunnish enemy. Heavy
have been the casualties on man and material, many and heavy the
losses inflicted on enemy crews and their machines; the quiet
fields and little copses have been strewn with smashed bodies and
splintered metal fragments. We have, it is hoped, established that
the Home Counties are not the least gracious and rich of the
English inheritance; let us appreciate them and cherish them
whatever they have suffered or may suffer at the hands of the
Herrenhöllenvolk. Much can be wiped out in a series of "Bae-
deker" raids, though if all the lost legions of the Luftwaffe were
recalled from the shades they could not expunge from these fair
counties their loveliness of nature, all their splendour of craftsmanship. But what matters it? Let them, as they have tried, lay in

* The Trefoil Publishing Co., 1931.

10 A DISTANT VIEW OF WINDSOR CASTLE

From a Watercolour by John Storer

the dust the stones of Canterbury Cathedral in the frustration of exasperated sadistic frenzy on the part of their blood-besotted maniacal degenerates,—the spirit that built Canterbury Cathedral remains unconquerable, and the building if crashed can rise again.

Let us stem the enemy's frantic futilities by the noble power of the 91st Psalm and the words of Luther:

> "And though this world with devils filled
> Shall threaten to undo us,
> We will not fear, for God hath willed
> His truth to triumph through us.
> Let goods and houses go
> This mortal life also
> God's truth abideth still
> And He will win the battle."

I must resist the temptation to set down once more the oft quoted words of William Morris, though in their insistence on the "little land" they are particularly applicable to the gentle contours and small-scale landscape of the Home Counties. Let us end by encouraging ourselves with the ever spring-fresh saying of Matthew Arnold, "The winding and deep lanes running out of the highroad on either side, the fresh and calm spots they take us to— how delicious it all is!" And as a summary we may find not inapplicable Dickens' sentences, originally penned about Hertfordshire, "Down among the pleasant dales and trout-streams of a green English county. No matter what county. Enough that you may traverse long grass-grown Roman roads there, open unknown barrows there, see many a square mile of richly cultivated land there and hold Arcadian talk with a bold peasantry, their country's pride, who will tell you (if you want to know) how pastoral housekeeping is done on a few shillings a week."

LITTLE BRAXTED CHURCH
Drawn by George Buckler

II

BOX HILL TO GUILDFORD

It is not only the pilgrims bound along the crescent chalk downs from Winchester to pay homage at the shrine of St. Thomas á Becket at Canterbury who used to tread the wide soft turf that overlooks the wooded weald of the South Country. There was yesterday an even larger exodus of pilgrims from London on the north along the valley of the Mole seeking wide vistas, sward to lie on, and quiet paths to walk. These climb up the steep slippery slopes above the *Burford Bridge* Hotel where Nelson stayed, and Keats came to finish *Endymion*.

> For by one step the blue sky should'st thou find
> And by another in deep sea below,
> See, through the trees, a little river go
> All in its midday gold and glimmering.

A little way up the slope at the edge of the trees stands Flint Cottage, where George Meredith wrote *Love in the Valley*, from which we look across the narrow valley to that sweetly named house Camilla Lacey, built by Fanny Burney, Johnson's sprightly gossiping little dear. Further up the hill we leave the slippery close-cropped grass for the many labyrinthine tracks through the woods of box that give this famous hill its name. On the summit of this hill, 700 ft. above sea level, is a view point marked with a guide to visitors showing the direction and distance of places as far afield as Crowborough and Shoreham Gap, that cleft in the South Downs through which on certain sunny days men claim that they can see the shining waters of the English Channel.

Eastward the Pilgrims' Way winds along the crest and sides of the downs towards red-roofed Reigate.

Our way lies westward, just down into the old market-town of Dorking, with its ancient gabled posting-houses of *The White Horse* and *The Red Lion*, and tall new pinnacled church with its memorial to Bishop Wilberforce ("Soapy Sam") who was killed here in 1873 as the result of a fall from his horse. There is an infinite choice of paths for the wayfarer on his journey to Guildford, for the pilgrims of old followed no one track. Some prefer the lovely wooded ways over high-lying Ranmore Common and Netley Heath. Others, and I think the wiser, make a wide detour in the valley of Holmesdale southwards to Wotton, where in the church, with its louvred Welsh border type tower, lie not only John Evelyn the diarist but all his family, in a chapel that is always kept scrupulously locked against the curious. To compensate for this, however, is the open path that leads past the house where the

11   THE WEATHERBOARDED WATERMILL ON THE LEA, LEMSFORD, HERTFORDSHIRE

12 AN UPLAND STRETCH ON THE CHALK DOWNLAND NEAR HEYDON, NORTH-WEST ESSEX

diarist was born, to plunge into pine woods that are reminiscent of the Highlands in their depth and wildness, up a track that follows an enchanting stream opening out into a little mere fringed by trees at the hamlet of Friday Street, where among the timbered and brick cottages stands one tiny inn mis-spelt *Stephen Langton*. The defile narrows still more as we climb up, still under the pines, until we emerge on waste lands of bracken, heather and gorse that would have called forth execration from Cobbett, but from those who have been long in city pent are greeted only with relief and delight. High up on the crest of this sandstone escarpment stands the tower of Leith Hill, to mark the only spot in the South-East of England where a man may, if he climbs over 34 ft. up its tower, be a thousand feet above sea level. This tower, which is as famous a landmark to Surrey as Chanctonbury Ring is to Sussex (each can be seen from the other), was built *circ.* 1766 by one Richard Hull of Bristol, who lies beneath its floor. The land falls very steeply away to the south to the wooded hamlets of the Sussex weald (14). It is so happily placed that from it views may be had over ten counties, even Wiltshire being visible in clear weather.

Westward the way, not always easy to find, leads by way of Holmbury St. Mary and the sandy tracks of the wild sandy Hurt Wood northward to Abinger Hammer (16), which gets its name from the old hammer-ponds formed from wayside streams to supply water-power for the smelting of the iron ore when it was worked in these woodlands. In the main street among the weather-boarded, gabled and flint houses stands a curious clock with a "smith-jack" striking a bell with his hammer every hour.

A mile or two further on along the valley are the villages of Gomshall and Shere, which always appear in any list of the most picturesque villages of England.

This is partly due to the church of Shere, cruciform, with central tower and broach spire. It was Norman in its original simple cross layout, and has developed by later mediaeval additions in a remarkable and interesting way, as studied by the late Francis Bond, till we get the present dual nave and chancel arrangement. There is a massive oak door bearing the date 1626, a Purbeck marble font, several small brasses, a window with the coats-of-arms of the Brays of Tower Hill, and the Fyfields, and a magnificent Norman south porch of very heavily carved chalk, with Purbeck marble shafts.

The path leads on by a tiny bridge over the Tillingbourne opposite Albury Park, the seat of the Duchess of Northumberland, to the church built of brick in the Romanesque style by Henry Drummond in 1842. Near-by is the famous Silent Pool, where King John is supposed to have seen a lovely peasant girl bathing and to have driven her to drown herself. The water is said to be peculiarly cold and the pool haunted by the helpless maiden. The first story I have proved to be false, of the second I cannot speak with authority.

William Cobbett of course came here and rejoiced in the loveliness of this part of the valley of Holmesdale through which the Tillingbourne flows, but two things filled him with horrified amazement, and he has left us his feelings in what I shall always regard as the finest piece of denunciatory prose in the English language. We may indulge in a smile at his attitude to bank-notes, but we cannot but be impressed. Here it is :—

"I came over the high hill on the south of Guildford, and came down to Chilworth, and up the valley to Albury. I noticed, in my first Rural Ride, this beautiful valley, its hangers, its meadows, its hop-gardens, and its ponds. . . . This pretty valley of Chilworth has a run of water which comes out of the high hills, and which, occasionally, spreads into a pond; so that there is in fact a series of ponds connected by this run of water. This valley, which seems to have been created by a bountiful providence, as one of the choicest retreats of man; which seems formed for a scene of innocence and happiness, has been, by ungrateful man, so perverted as to make it instrumental in effecting two of the most damnable of purposes; in carrying into execution two of the most damnable inventions that ever sprang from the minds of man under the influence of the devil! namely, the making of gunpowder and of bank-notes! Here in this tranquil spot, where the nightingales are to be heard earlier and later in the year than in any other part of England; where the first bursting of the bud is seen in Spring, where no rigour of seasons can ever be felt; where everything seems formed for precluding the very thought of wickedness; here has the devil fixed on as one of the seats of his grand manufactory; and perverse and ungrateful man not only lends him his aid, but lends it cheerfully! As to the gunpowder, indeed, we might get over that. In some cases that may be innocently, and, when it sends the lead at the hordes that support a tyrant, meritoriously employed. The alders and the willows, therefore, one can see, without so much regret, turned into powder by the waters of this valley; but the Bank-notes! To think that the springs which God has commanded to flow from the sides of these happy hills, for the comfort and delight of man; to think that these springs should be perverted into means of spreading misery over a whole nation; and that, too, under the base and hypocritical pretence of promoting its credit and maintaining its honour and its faith. There was one circumstance indeed that served to mitigate the melancholy excited by these reflections; namely, that a part of these springs have, at times, assisted in turning rags into Registers! Somewhat cheered by the thought of this, but still, in a more melancholy mood than I had been for a long while, I rode on with my friend towards Albury, up the valley, the sandhills on one side of us, and the chalk hills on the other."

13   LOOKING TO THE NORTH DOWNS, WESTCOTT, NEAR DORKING

Drawn by M. and C. H. B. Quennell

LATE SEVENTEENTH CENTURY STAIRCASE IN A RESTAURANT IN
GUILDFORD HIGH STREET

Over the crest of the hill lies Newlands Corner, a splendid high
view point (15), with a house once the home of St. Loe Strachey,
and a broad green track leads past St. Martha's Chapel, where the
old pilgrims rested, to the ancient town of Guildford, the foundation stone of whose new cathedral was laid in 1936; it will cost
when completed £250,000.

Opposite the present Pro-Cathedral, the dignified red-brick
Georgian church of the Holy Trinity, stands Bishop Abbot's
Hospital of the Blessed Trinity, a fine Tudor building of red
brick, with lodgings for twelve brethren and eight sisters, all of
whom must be sixty years old before admission. Access is easy to
its old oak staircase, dining-hall with contemporary furniture and

D

Drawn by J. K. Colling

APSIDAL WALL PAINTINGS, ST. MARY'S, GUILDFORD

lovely board-room. Also in this famous thronged High Street, which is on the main Portsmouth Road, are the delightful little Guildhall built in 1683, with its louvréd turret and ornate projecting clock, the Grammar School of Edward VI's time and an inn, *The Lion*, where Pepys stayed and you may, surprisingly, see the original hunting horn of John Peel. One house, which has changed hands often and is now a restaurant, is contemporary with the Guildhall, and has a richly carved staircase with a scroll balustrade, and some very fine casement fasteners. Of the original Castle there still stands the 70 ft. high Norman Keep, with walls of flint and chalk 10 ft. thick and superstructure of ragstone and Roman

brick built in herring-bone fashion. There is a museum of local
country implements in the Castle gateway. The church of St.
Nicholas, completely rebuilt in 1875 in an unpleasant modern
version of alien Gothick, contains memorials of the Mores of
Loseley, but St. Mary's is, possibly after Compton, the most
interesting church in Surrey. The oldest part is the Pre-Conquest
Tower, by far the most striking monument of its period in the
county. At the end of the twelfth century the Pre-Conquest nave
and chancel were removed and the present church erected with a
very rare tri-apsidal East End. The central apse was destroyed to
make room for the coach of George, Prince of Wales, who wished
for a wider way to Brighton. There are wall-paintings, still fine
though faded and fragmentary, showing St. John seated in a
cauldron of boiling oil, held down with a pitch-fork, raising
Drusiana of Ephesus to life, and turning sticks and stones into gold
and jewels. We see him drinking without hurt from a poisoned
cup, which has already taken its effect on two men lying dead at
his feet. There is St. John the Baptist, with a rope round his neck
before Herod, and afterwards beheaded, the executioner's hair
standing on end and hands upraised in horror. There is also a
picture of St. Michael holding a balance, which a devil is trying to
press down so that the weighed soul may kick the beam, and of
damned souls being carted off in bundles to be burnt in hell.

But it is neither of the very old Guildford nor of the very new
with its fine lido, by-pass roads and unfinished Cathedral that I
first think, but of the Guildford of Cobbett's day. "Taken with its
environs," he says, "I who have seen so many, many towns, think
it the prettiest, and taken altogether, the most agreeable and most
happy looking that I ever saw in my life. Here are hill and dale in
endless variety. Here are the chalk and the sand, vying with each
other in making beautiful scenes. Here is a navigable river and
fine meadows. Here are woods and downs. Here is something of
everything but flat marshes and their skeleton-making agues."
Eric Parker, who knows his England as well as any of us, de-
scribes Guildford High Street as a model of what the main Street
of an English town should be. It is only fair to add that he was
speaking of forty years ago, when it was truer than it is today, as
it now has to cope with more vehicles than any High Street
should be called upon to tackle, in spite of the by-passing through
side streets of much of the Portsmouth Road and Farnham traffic.

III

GUILDFORD TO SELBORNE

"Everybody," says Cobbett, "that has been from Goldalming to
Guildford knows that there is hardly another such a pretty four
miles in all England. The road is good: the houses are neat: the
people are neat: the hills, the woods, the meadows all are beautiful. Nothing wild and bold, to be sure, but exceedingly pretty:
and it is almost impossible to ride along these four miles without
feelings of pleasure, though you have rain for your companion, as
it happened to be with me."

Both the main routes out of Guildford, westward over the
Hog's Back, and under its lee to Godalming are full of interest.
From the bare ridge of the Hog's Back the view northward is over
the little heaths and fields of Normandy, where Cobbett lived in
later life, to Aldershot and the black ridges of Caesar's Camp or
Laffan's Plain. But southward where the Pilgrims' Way runs there
are many hidden treasures among the steep woods. Notably there
is the grey Tudor house of Loseley, built by Sir William More
from the stones of Waverley Abbey and still the house of that
famous family. Here Queen Elizabeth, James I and Charles I
found rich entertainment, and from here young Anne, daughter of
Sir George More, ran away with the poet John Donne, afterwards
Dean of St. Paul's. It was here that Elizabeth imprisoned Henry
Wriothesley, Earl of Southampton, who was Shakespeare's
intimate friend. The long front with its serried gables, square
projecting bays and many-light Tudor windows, is dignified and
impressive; the interiors are of Early Renaissance richness,
especially the drawing-room with its elaborately carved chimney-
piece of chalk; they are depicted in Nash's *Mansions of England*.
The manuscripts of the Muniment Room are of great historical
interest, especially for the Tudor and Stuart period.

Within a mile or so of this famous house is an even more
famous church, that of Compton, which is hardly to be equalled
for interest in all England. The building, which is mainly late
Transitional, contains the only double, two-storeyed chancel in the
Kingdom (21); it is really a chantry chapel built immediately over
the altar, opening towards the church. This chantry, which is
reached by a wooden stair, contains a wooden balustrade of nine
semi-circular arches, the only piece of Norman wooden screen
work remaining in this country. The shingled spired tower is
supposed to date from the days of Edward the Confessor, while
the font is twelfth century; the pulpit, altar-rails and chancel
screen are all Jacobean. There is also a fragment of stained glass
dating as far back as 1175. Compton is furthermore fortunate in a
rector whose enthusiasm for his church leads him to be ever ready
to unfold its wonders to interested visitors. Close by is a strange
looking terra-cotta chapel of original type erected to the memory

of G. F. Watts, containing remarkable symbolic plaster decoration and paintings.

At Puttenham we find an attractive place of commons and pleasant old cottages with a long narrow lake, and in the large Park of Hampton is a twefth century church with a fifteenth century tower, mysterious arch and several good brasses, one to Edward Crawford, priest (died 1431) being singularly perfect. Here too, is a Tudor House with projecting porch and room over it called "Shoelands." Just to the south on a high plateau are the Victorian brick towers of Charterhouse; the school, Thackeray's Greyfriars, moved from London some seventy years ago.

Godalming in the valley of the Wey just below, the birthplace of General Oglethorpe the founder of the colony of Georgia, where the Wesleys worked, is as ancient as it is lovely. The most notable feature of the town is the lofty leaded spire of its church, one of the largest and finest in the county. There is good thirteenth and fourteenth century work, a sixteenth century doorway and some Saxon carved stone.

In Charles II's reign the town was used as a hunting box, and in the eighteenth century developed into a wool centre. *The King's Arms* has many royal memories, for Alexander I of Russia dined here with the King of Prussia, and in Queen Anne's reign Peter the Great ordered a gargantuan breakfast and dinner for himself and retinue of twenty courtiers.

Godalming was also the home of that astonishing woman Mary Tofts, who claimed to have given birth to several litters of rabbits, which accounted for a widespread distaste for them as food until her fabrications were rewarded by imprisonment.

Two other features of the town deserve especial notice, the long, low, red brick almshouses founded in 1622 by Richard Wyatt who was three times Lord Mayor of London, and the often photographed 700 year old bridge that spans the Wey at Eashing.

Close by is the fine deer park of Peperharow, the seat of Lord Midleton with magnificent cedars, chestnuts, oaks and beeches and a little church remodelled in 1850 by Augustus Pugin, surrounded by cypresses, yews and junipers and containing many interesting brasses. The neighbouring village of Elstead, supposed to have been the steading of Ella, founder of the Kingdom of Sussex, has a little thirteenth century church with huge tie-beams in the nave roof, a solid timber belfry-stair and a panelled chest. Elstead also boasts a green, an ancient bridge over the Wey and a mill. On the other side of Crooksbury Hill with its fine pine trees, stands the lovely little village of Seale with red-roofed cottages standing above green meadows, hop gardens and oast houses. The church has a fourteenth century timber porch, and a Norman font, but little else of interest owing to savage restoration.

We are now on the threshold of the most fascinating corner in all Surrey, the ruins of Waverley Abbey and the historic house of Moor Park. Waverley, the earliest Cistercian Abbey in England, eldest sister of Tintern, was founded in 1128 by William Giffard, Bishop of Winchester, but a great storm carried away the greater part of it in 1201. In 1215 the well-water dried up, and in 1233 and 1265 two more storms threatened to sweep it away. It was not till 1278 that it was dedicated, and the ceremonial revels, which lasted for nine days, were attended by 7,066 guests. At the Dissolution Sir William More of Loseley was one of the principal vandals to cart away the stones to build other secular houses. So today we have to content ourselves with a few broken-down walls, windows and doorways.

Moor Park, on the other hand, a little way along the wooded hilly valley, stands gloriously intact. It came just into prominence when Sir William Temple, foreign secretary to William III, brought his wife, the enchanting Royalist girl Dorothy Osborne of Chicksands, to share a long and happy life with him there. After the long separation of the Civil War they lived to a ripe old age in this enchanting country, laying out their garden—Temple's essay on Gardens is as famous as Bacon's—and harbouring for a while one of the greatest geniuses in the language.

Jonathan Swift was scarcely more than a boy when he came as secretary of Temple and gave promise of his intellectual prowess by writing here *A Tale of a Tub* and *The Battle of the Books*. The little hill up and down which he used to run for his daily exercise still stands, as does the little cottage where he spent so much time with his dearly beloved Stella, to whom in after years he wrote his famous Stella's Journal. Her real name was Esther Johnson. She was the daughter of Sir William's steward, and cited as Sewing-maid to Lady Giffard, Temple's sister. The relationship between Swift and this young girl remains a mystery. She became his constant companion, and her death completely broke him up, but whether he ever married her and if he didn't, why he didn't, has given rise to many conjectures, none of which has been proved.

Another ghost of a very different sort haunts these sandy paths and woodland glades, the doughty champion of the farm labourer, William Cobbett, author of *Rural Rides*. He was born close by in *The Jolly Farmer* inn at Farnham on the 9th March 1762. Let him speak for himself:—

"There is a little hop garden in which I used to work when from eight to ten years old: from which I have run scores of times to follow the hounds, leaving the hoe to do the best it could to destroy the weeds: but the most interesting thing was a sand-hill which goes from a part of the heath down to the rivulet of the Bourn.

"I, with my two brothers used to go to the top of the hill, which was steeper than the roof of a house: one used to draw his arms out of the sleeves of his smock-frock, and lay himself down with his arms by his sides: and then the others, one at head and the other at feet, sent him rolling down the hill like a barrel or a log of wood.

"I had often told my sons of this when they were very little, and I now took one of them to see the spot. This was the spot where I was receiving my education, and I am perfectly satisfied that if I had not received such an education, if I had been brought up as a milk-sop, with a nursery-maid everlastingly at my heels, I should have been at this day as great a fool, as inefficient a mortal, as any of those frivolous idiots that are turned out from Winchester school, or from any of those dens of dunces called colleges and universities. It is impossible to say how much I owe to that sand hill, and I went to return it my thanks for the utility which it probably gave me to be one of the greatest terrors to one of the greatest and most powerful bodies of knaves and fools that ever were permitted to afflict this or any other country."

Cobbett gives us a graphic account of a visit with his eleven year old son to the ruins of Waverley Abbey to show him where he used to gather and to eat a variety of strawberries known as hautboys, a tree out of which he fell into the river while trying to rob a crow's nest, an elm tree where he saw a cat as large as a spaniel—a story that was disbelieved but to which he stuck in spite of a beating,—Mother Ludlum's hole all gone to rack and ruin, the little hill up and down which Swift (one of his earliest heroes) went for his run, and the place where Sir William Temple's heart was buried under a garden seat that he looked for in vain.

You will find no more entertaining guide to Surrey or any other county than this downright, plain-spoken farmer's son who at the age of eleven ran away from Farnham with 6½d. in his pocket and slept under a haystack in Richmond, his last threepence spent on a copy of *A Tale of a Tub* which he still carried with him in later years when he enlisted as a soldier and went out to America. His *Rural Rides* is a classic, in which he comments in vigorous racy English on the country and the state of its farming, and nobly champions the cause of the agricultural worker. Everything in this neighbourhood seems to be overshadowed by Cobbett, but Farnham, one of Surrey's most picturesque towns has many other points of first rate interest.

First, towering above the old wide street, is the famous castle of the Bishop of Winchester (18), with its fine brick gateway tower built in in the sixteenth century by Bishop Fox, and its memories of many Royal visits from the days of Edward I to Queen Victoria. It was here that Queen Elizabeth warned the Duke of Norfolk not to marry Mary Queen of Scots.

During the Civil War the poet George Wither held it for the Roundheads, but as he met with no response to his demand for guns, he had no alternative but to surrender it to another poet, Sir John Denham, who in his turn had to give it up to a third poet, Sir William Waller. When Wither was later taken prisoner by the Royalists, Denham successfully begged for his life, on the sporting and unusual grounds that while Wither lived he, Denham, would not be the worst poet in England. The castle was ultimately "slighted", but at the Restoration again made habitable at a cost of £2,000, Bishop Morley (1662–1682) spending a further £11,000 on its improvement, but contenting himself with a tiny cell, a stone couch to sleep on, without fire summer or winter, and living on one meal a day. As he lived to be 87 he provides a good argument for the healthiness of an ascetic life. It was in Farnham castle while he was the guest of Bishop Morley that Isaak Walton wrote the lives of Hooker and George Herbert. Morley's fine Carolean panelled staircase hall makes an impressive interior.

Farnham was also the life-long home of the novelist Edna Lyall, and the birthplace of Toplady, the author of "Rock of Ages", who described Wesley as "an old fox tarred and feathered", and died at 38. In the churchyard is the massive tomb of William Cobbett, and the restored cruciform parish church of St. Andrew shares with Croydon the honour of being one of the two largest in the county. It is partly twelfth century and possesses a good octagonal font, fine fifteenth century sedilia and piscina, classical altar rails and several good brasses.

A few miles over the Hampshire border, none too easy to find, among the deep winding lanes and wooded hangers is Selborne, the home of Gilbert White, most informative and entertaining of naturalists. Once more let Cobbett be our guide.

"At Tisted I crossed the turn-pike road and entered a lane which at the end of about four miles brought me to Selborne.

"When I got within half a mile of this village I came suddenly to the edge of a hill where Hindhead and Black Down came full in my view. The Itchen, Wey and Arun rise here.

"The village of Selborne is precisely what it is described by Mr. White, a straggling, irregular street bearing all the marks of great antiquity. It is very beautiful. Nothing can surpass in beauty these dells and hillocks and hangers, which last are so steep that it is impossible to ascend them, except by means of a serpentine path.

"I found here deep hollow Ways, with beds and sides of solid white stone.

"The churchyard is most beautifully situated. I measured the yew tree in the churchyard (how typical that is of precise Cobbett) and found the trunk to be, according to my measurements 23 ft. 8 ins. in circumference. I have never seen such quantity of grapes upon any vines as I have seen upon the vines in this village."

What Cobbett omits to tell us is that the inscription on White's simple grave, which is very difficult to find, must be the most modest ever put on the tombstone of a famous man. It runs simply "G.W. 26 June 1793." In the church however, there is a new stained glass memorial window put in by admirers on both sides of the Atlantic. There are also monuments to another Gilbert White, grandfather of the naturalist, fellow of Magdalen College, Oxford, which still owns the property. Gilbert the author was born in the vicarage in 1720, but settled in a house called "The

15   LOOKING SOUTHWARD AT NEWLANDS CORNER, NEAR GUILDFORD

15   HOMESTEADS AT ABINCER HAMMER, NEAR GUILDFORD

17 THE RUINS OF NEWARK PRIORY BY THE WEY, SURREY

18 THE GEORGIAN STREET OF FARNHAM AND THE CASTLE, SURREY

Drawn by Sydney R. Jones

SELBORNE FROM THE HANGER

Wakes'" which still remains. Near-by stands the home of yet
another famous author, Jane Austen, who lived at Chawton, but
as we have already strayed beyond the Home Counties we must
set our course once more eastwards.

E

IV

LEITH HILL TO SELBORNE BY WAY OF HINDHEAD

THE whole country in this district is full of hills and dales, wild wastes of bracken and heather, interspersed with thick woods, with unexpected streams and at times large sheets of water. It is ideal walking country, particularly round Haslemere and Hindhead.

In Haslemere church is a memorial window by Burne-Jones to Tennyson, to remind us that the poet lived at Aldworth on Blackdown, the highest point of Sussex, still a secluded wooded height, from which there are grand views all over the western weald of Sussex to the wooded South Downs. George Eliot wrote *Middlemarch* at Brookbank Cottage, Shottermill, a place of pleasant ponds, and not far away we come to that long succession of hidden waters known as Waggoners Wells, a property bought for the nation by friends of Sir Robert Hunter.

But the main attraction in this neighbourhood is the Devil's Punch Bowl at Hindhead (20), as wild and desolate a height as you will find in the South of England, and full of reminders of Scotland. There are traces of the old road, now just a sandy track, which climbed steeply up Gibbet Hill, where a tall cross of Cornish granite marks a spot 895 ft. above sea-level where three tramps were hanged in chains for the murder of a sailor in 1786. This was described by Cobbett as "the most villainous spot God ever made", but Cobbett as we know judged land by its fertility and not from its wild beauty or wide views.

And the view is without doubt one of the finest, if not the finest in all the Home Counties, for it stretches away to the north over the ridge of the Hog's Back to ridge upon ridge as far as Berkshire, with a suspicion even of London to the north-east, while to the south beyond the wooded slopes of Black Down rises the long clean line of the smooth South Downs and the high chalk hills that protect Portsmouth. In the foreground fall away the heather-covered commons with the tumbledown cottages of the broom-squires and the cone-shaped humps of the Devil's Jumps at Thursley. In every direction there are grand walks. One of the most pleasant winds its way through Churt, the home of Mr. Lloyd George, by way of Frensham, with its magnificent Great Pond of 108 acres, well stocked with eels, perch, carp and pike, which by reason of its sandy shore looms like an inland sea (24).

To the east of Frensham lies the village of Thursley with hammer-ponds, picturesque common, and a church with magnificent beams. Near-by is the extensive park of Witley, with its commons of some 375 acres, bequeathed to the National Trust in 1927. The church at Witley, cruciform, with central tower and

By courtesy of Oliver Hill, Esq.

19   A TILE-HUNG SURREY HOMESTEAD: VALWOOD FARM NEAR HASLEMERE

20   THE DEVIL'S PUNCHBOWL, HINDHEAD, SURREY

shingled spire, has beautiful tracery in its fourteenth century east
window, a thirteenth century octagonal font, and a painting that
has been claimed as Saxon. But the cream of this country, and
much the least known, lies on the other side of the Southern
Railway line, where lie the many villages ending in "fold"—
Chiddingfold, Dunsfold, Alfold and the rest, to the south of
Hambledon. Chiddingfold, in particular, is a quiet lovely hamlet
of fine well built houses, with a half timber and tile-hung inn, *The
Crown* (22), first built in the reign of Richard II, whose title-deed
dated 22nd March 1383 assigns the hall and the chamber for a
rental of four shillings a year. The church, which is late twelfth
century, has been over-restored. At one time Chiddingfold was a
centre of the glass-making furnaces, which were suppressed by
Elizabeth as a nuisance. Dunsfold, with cottages scattered round a
wide green, has a beautiful little cruciform church built at the end
of the thirteenth century, with exquisite window tracery and
mouldings and a dozen fifteenth century pews, the ends of which
are shaped into curves at the top. Alfold church has a Norman
font, a Jacobean carved pulpit, massive timber framing to its little
fifteenth century western tower, a fine yew in the churchyard and
some old stocks at the gate. This was a remarkable district for
glass manufacture in the Middle Ages, and possibly earlier. Some
archaeologists have, by painstaking research, unearthed the sites
of a number of kilns, with fascinating and valuable remains of the
processes, materials and products.

Here is one of the most densely wooded tracts in the Home
or any other group of counties: the sandy stretches and the clay
lands of the Weald have each their own growths, but are so mixed
up that they combine to produce a wide and varied range of tree
and shrub. There are widely extending coppices of hazel or
hawthorn, thickets of scrub oak, scattered belts of pine, slopes of
furze, bracken and heather. Between Dunsfold and Alfold are
dense oakwoods which form a remnant of the old *Anderida Sylva*.
In spring, under the masses of tossing yellow catkins the new
green-clad soil is starred with myriad wild anemones and dotted
with primrose clumps; late in autumn the dark tones of fir and
gorse contrast with the russet of bracken and young oaks, which,
like their youthful beech cousins, keep their leaves all through the
leafless months.

Just north of this retiring modest "fold" stretch, there is some
splendid hill country between Hambledon and the wooded hill of
Hascombe, the crown of which is covered with especial fine
beeches. Below in the valley lies the busy little market town of
Cranleigh, famous for its Public School and the Elizabethan house
of Baynards Park, built in 1577 by Sir George More of Loseley.
Here is kept the old charter chest of Sir Thomas More, and it was
to this home that his daughter, Margaret Roper, brought his head
before taking it to Canterbury. Cranleigh church is a fine cruci-

form building of the twelfth–fourteenth centuries with three
beautiful sedilia and a large piscina, traceried pulpit, fifteenth
century screen, a most unusual octagonal Transitional font, and
massive pillars. This district is very rich in large red brick country
houses, each standing in its own park among great trees. They
mostly date from the late nineteenth century and are often placed
in the vale between two hills of a ridge. An amateur flying photo-
grapher some years ago recorded some scores of them from his
plane; they made an impressive series of estates, which bore
witness to the popularity of South-west Surrey among successful
men, but many of the houses were not free from the typical varied
faults of their period.

Over the fields northward, lying under the lee of Coneyhurst or
Pitch Hill, which vies in glory with that of Leith but is much less
well known (23), is the charming village of Ewhurst with in the
aisleless church, badly restored, a Georgian communion table and
fine three-sided rails, good Jacobean pulpit, old king-post roof,
and very remarkable fourteenth century font.

After climbing the steep pine-covered sandy slopes of Coneyhurst, we are once more on the Leith Hill sandy forest ridge, and
our circular tour completed as soon as we have found our way
across the open heathy tracts of gorse and bracken, through
glades of pine and scrub oak, over Holmbury Hill,—the middle
sister, in position, and at 857 ft. in height, of the trio of the Leith
Hill range,—which we have already skirted at Holmbury St.
Mary or Felday, as it is sometimes called. The village, largely
modern, is beautifully situated, and the pleasant simple church was
designed and built by George Edmund Street, who was responsible for the London Law Courts, with a window in memory of
his second wife.

Drawn by J. Tavenor Perry

BREWER STREET FARMHOUSE, BLETCHINGLEY (v. p. 31)

V

DORKING TO TUNBRIDGE WELLS

IF you want to keep away from the haunts of men you will walk along the crest of the chalk hills from Box Hill by way of Betchworth Camp, with superb views southward all the way, and wide secluded tracts of woodland and heather running off to the north.

But along the winding banks of the Mole in the valley below are many picturesque villages and points of interest that must make the traveller pause before deciding to stay on the high ground all the time. Just east of Dorking, for instance, is Betchworth Park with a walk open across it; here stood the castle that was fortified in 1449, pulled down in 1700 and acquired by the owner of the adjoining estate of The Deepdene, where later lived his son Thomas Hope, the famous neo-Grec designer and dilletante, collector of sculpture and author of *Anastasius*. It was recently sold and the house became for a time a private hotel.

Beyond the village of Brockham lies Betchworth, famous for its oft painted chalk pit, with its weatherboarded timbered inn *The Red Lion* and church in which is a brass to William Wardysworth (vicar 1533) and a huge monoxylon Norman oak chest. A little to the south is Leigh (pronounced "Lie",) a Wealden hamlet with a green, timbered cottages roofed with Horsham stone, and fine brasses in the church to the Arderne family of Leigh Place, of which the original moat remains, but the house has been largely rebuilt. This was once the seat of the famous Braose family, then came Sir Thomas de Arderne, who, coveting Margery, wife of Nicholas de Poynings, murdered her husband and married her. She died of a broken heart, and her ghost is said still to haunt the house. One of the later owners, Sir Thomas Coley, was accused by Elizabeth of using titles to which he had no right. The ridge of the North Downs above these places sweeps along at a full 700 ft., and from several vantage points—Betchworth clump, Colley Hill, Reigate Hill, affords us to the south a succession of breath-taking views.

Across the wide heath to the north-east, where stands an ancient windmill converted into a chapel, is the ancient busy market town of Reigate on the Brighton Road. In the restored church are monuments to Sir Thomas Bludder, 1619, Richard Elyot and boy and an ugly effigy of Richard Ladbroke, 1730. The monument to Howard of Effingham, who was buried at sea in 1624, was not erected till 1888.

Reigate Priory, pleasant, low and Georgian, built in 1779, occupies the site of the house in which Lord Howard's father lived, founded originally by de Warenne in the thirteenth century as a Priory of Austin Canons. The old castle of Reigate, which occupied a very strong strategic position on the Pilgrims' Way, surrendered to Louis of France when he pursued King John to Winchester in 1216, and de Warenne, its owner, had to change sides before he got it back. After the battle of Lewes he had to escape to France, but when de Montfort fell at Evesham, he regained it.

Redhill, which is entirely modern, is of no particular interest, but just beyond it is Nutfield, famous for its Fuller's earth, one of the oldest of industries, its export being forbidden as far back as the reign of Edward II. Reigate also has a curious little out of the way industry—the quarrying of hearthstones, which go to all parts. There is an old posting-house, *The Queen's Head*, and the thirteenth century church has a fifteenth century tower with a short shingled spire, many good brasses, and a very fine Tudor pulpit. Down in the clayey land below stands the most famous windmill in England, that of Outwood from which in 1666 the miller saw the great fire of London, and in which his descendants still grind the corn as they have for three hundred years in unbroken succession. There are two mills close together on the Common.

North of Redhill and Nutfield on the main road and rail is Merstham, where there is a well proportioned and effective Early English and Perpendicular church, with a number of noteworthy features including a number of mildly interesting brasses.

The sandy stretch due east of Redhill swells into a sharply-defined but interrupted ridge, over which the east-west Holmes-dale road is carried, threading the villages of Nutfield, Bletchingley, and as it trends farther north, Godstone, Limpsfield and Oxted. At just over 600 ft. these spots enjoy prospects to the south over the Weald scarcely less than those of the highest points of the chalk, and northward they command the long range of the North Downs far in each direction.

Close to Nutfield on the sandy heights is the very interesting and picturesque village of Bletchingley, with a fine old inn, *The White Hart*, and a church famous for its bells. In 1789 the ringers rang a full peal of 5,600 changes in 3 hours 36 mins. In this church there is a huge monument to an eighteenth century Lord Mayor of London, Sir Robert Clayton, described by Dryden as "as good a saint as usurer ever made." He owned the castle which formerly belonged to Anne of Cleves and later to Sir Thomas Cawarden who entertained Henry VIII there, but on the accession of Mary was arrested for using it as an armoury. It was once in the possession of the Howards of Effingham and of Elizabeth, Countess of Peterborough, whose son under the Commonwealth was fined £10,000 for turning Roman Catholic, which necessitated its sale to Sir Robert Clayton. One of the rectors of Bletchingley, Thomas Herring, inveighed strongly from his pulpit against the demoral-

22   THE CROWN INN, CHIDDINGFOLD, SURREY

21   THE DOUBLE CHANCEL, COMPTON CHURCH, SURREY

23   THE SOUTH-WESTERN VIEW FROM PITCH HILL, EWHURST, LOOKING TO BLACKDOWN AND HINDHEAD
THE NEARER HEIGHT BETWEEN IS HASCOMBE HILL

ising effect of *The Beggar's Opera* and because of this, or perhaps in spite of it, ended as Archbishop of Canterbury. An earlier rector, Dr. Harris, an ardent politician in Charles I's reign had to kneel at the bar of the House of Commons in contrition for canvassing for a Member who was elected by bribery. The last member of what Cobbett called "this vile rotten borough" was Lord Palmerston. Pendell is a good early Later-Renaissance house, and Brewer Street Farmhouse (p. 28) a fine twin gabled timber structure.

Cobbett was more polite about the adjoining township of Godstone which he rightly described as "A beautiful village, chiefly of one street with a fine large green before it, and with a pond on the green." It is particularly rich in ancient and picturesque inns, *The Clayton Arms*, once called *The White Hart*, being a favourite resting place of Cobbett who specially liked the garden and the surrounding woods, coppices and ponds. The church which has been enlarged or restored by Sir Gilbert Scott, has a number of monuments to the Evelyn family and his wife Dame Thomasin. Scott also put up some quite pleasant half-timber almshouses which may compare with George Devey's cottages by Penshurst Churchyard (p. 34).

Just beyond Tandridge where there was once a priory and still is a famous yew tree over 32 ft. in circumference, comes Oxted, just on the Kent border, a village of little inns, notably *The Bell*, timber and brick cottages with stone steps, gables and dormer windows, and a church with a squat fourteenth century tower, octagonal fifteenth century font, tiny oak staircase with rails and balustrade of late seventeenth century, and brasses to two children of the Hoskin family.

To reach Tunbridge Wells from Oxted we here leave the line of the chalk hills and make a plunge southward to Crowhurst, which has an even more famous yew tree than Tandridge (25), as fourteen people can sit, and presumably have sat, at table in its interior. It is about 33 ft. round. Crowhurst Place, lately renovated, is a fine, half timber early Tudor house of local type with panelled interiors and an impressive moat. The church has a fifteenth century tall wooden spire (25) and many monuments to the Gagnesford family dating from 1450 to 1591.

Due south again is Lingfield which has other claims to fame beyond its race-course. It is a village of brick and timber cottages, with a fifteenth century shop front, a pond on the banks of which, built on to the bole of an old oak, stands a strange stone cage, from which the Copthorne poachers were once rescued. The cruciform church was rebuilt in 1431 by the second Lord Cobham, who converted it into a college, which was suppressed by Henry VIII; the cloister and court in the seventeenth century were described by Aubrey as nearly perfect. There are a chained sixteenth century Bible, fifteenth century stalls, and a fine screen, but the outstanding feature of the church is its monuments. There is

Drawn by Sydney R. Jones

CROWHURST PLACE, BEFORE RENOVATION

an effigy of Reginald, first Lord Cobham, wearing the Garter on his left leg, a brass of Reginald, second Lord Cobham, 1403, an alabaster tomb with effigies of the third Lord, 1417, a brass to Elizabeth Stoker, maid of honour to the first Lady Cobham, brasses to two provosts of the College, and many monuments to the Howards of Effingham. Of Sterborough Castle, the home of the Cobhams, only the moat remains. It was here that Louis Bourbon was imprisoned after being taken prisoner at Agincourt. In the Civil war it was garrisoned by the Roundheads and "slighted" by them.

The first Lord Cobham was one of the three knights to whom the Black Prince was entrusted at Crecy. He rescued the King of France at Poitiers, became Lord Admiral and died of the plague. His wife, Joan, is remarkable for having made one of the longest wills ever known, in which she left 7,000 pence for 7,000 masses to be said for her soul, a twelve years' undertaking. The second Lord tried to secure a dispensation from the Pope for marrying his cousin. As penance, the couple were compelled to do without meat for four years, to go without wine on Wednesdays, and not only to feed four persons daily but to wait on them in person. It was his son who founded the College, and his daughter Eleanor became the wife of Duke Humphrey of Gloucester, and was accused of using sorcery and enchantment to put him on the throne.

We are now in a pocket of very considerable historic and scenic

24   FRENSHAM GREAT POND, SURREY

25   HARVEST BY CROWHURST CHURCH, SURREY
THE FAMOUS YEW TREE IS ON THE LEFT OF THE CHURCH

26   LOOKING ACROSS THE EDEN VALLEY TO THE NORTH DOWNS FROM A LANE NEAR EDENBRIDGE

interest, for close by are Hever Castle, the lovely villages Chiddingstone and Groombridge, and Penshurst Place.

First then Hever, famous for its castle and associations with Henry VIII and Anne Boleyn; the village with its *Henry VIII* inn is on the Eden, which feeds the castle moat and is turned to ornamental account in the grounds. The church, on a neighbouring hill, stands out for its tall shingled spire; it is largely Decorated, but the Boleyn chantry chapel is late Perpendicular; there are several brasses, one of them a very fine effigy on an altar tomb to Sir Thomas Bullen, Anne's father, 1538; he is richly apparelled as a Knight of the Garter.

The castle, which is a perfect example of a castellated and moated house, built at a period when comfort as well as security was sought after, was the place of Anne's education under Simonette, her French 'gouvernante'; she went to France in the train of Mary Tudor, and it was here that Henry VIII found her when he had lost his way hawking, seized upon her like one of his own hawks, made her Queen of England, and mother of Queen Elizabeth. Several letters of affection he wrote her to the castle are still extant. The roads of Hever had as evil a name as any in Sussex, and the tradition has it that Henry VIII, on his way to the castle, would sometimes find himself literally and abundantly "stuck in the mud", and the retainers would sally out with torches to extricate him at the sound of his hunting horn. The building is quadrangular with a medieval core and much haphazard but not ineffective Tudor addition. The gatehouse, with its machicolations, drawbridge, two restored but still working portcullises, flanked by two stern loopholed towers, wears an air of businesslike defence. The old hall, the dining hall, Anne Boleyn's bedroom and the long gallery still remain intact. The first Lord Astor restored the place and added to it sympathetically, and laid out, regardless of expense, splendid gardens of great extent with numberless attractive features. But all this and the castle itself are entirely secluded from the ordinary traveller's view.

But if Hever is hidden there is full compensation in the exquisite village of Chiddingstone, which is not only open to the public gaze, but the property of the public, for it belongs to the National Trust, and the beauty of its Tudor Street can never be desecrated.

The quiet village street of half-timbered gabled cottages with dormer and mullioned windows, varying in date from the reign of Henry VII to Elizabeth, remains quite unspoilt, and its charm is enhanced by the trees of the neighbouring park above, and the cobbled causeway that runs below the projecting windows.

The church standing a little back among exceptionally fine trees has a tall Perpendicular tower with octagonal turrets and crocketed pinnacles, and a south porch dated 1626, with an unusual combination of Gothick and Renaissance work, apparently contemporary with the pulpit and font. There are two iron

F

gravestones in the interior, one commemorating Richard Streat-feild, who died here in 1601. The manor house of the Streatfeilds, who have held this property for nearly 450 years and still live there, stands close by the church in a large park, in which stands the famous boulder of sandstone, known as the chiding stone, locally assumed to be originally a Druid judgment stone.

A charming walk over the fields leads to Penshurst Place, the castellated Tudor house of Sir Philip Sidney, rising above smooth green lawns with no obstructive hedge or fence to hide any of its naked glory. It has been best described by its most famous tenant. "Built", says Sir Philip Sidney in *Arcadia* of fair and strong stone, not affecting so much any extraordinary kind of fineness as an honourable representing of a firm stateliness, handsome without curiosity and homely without loathsomeness." Its treasures accu-mulated through the centuries are infinite, but perhaps its out-standing glory is the very lofty fourteenth century great Hall, the span of whose timber roof is exceeded only by that of West-minster. This roof is 60 ft. high, and that is of the kingpost and collar-beam type, richly moulded and supported by great curved braces, carried down to the wall-plate. This hall is 54 ft. long and 39 ft. wide, and still retains the hearth in the centre, which was never replaced by a fireplace and chimney (27); the old trestle tables and a fifteenth century screen and gallery. Other notable rooms are the long Gallery, filled with famous portraits—Queen Elizabeth's room which is finely panelled. It is an almost perfect example of a mediaeval country house, built less for defence than for comfort.

Its first owners were the de Penchesters, one of whom, Stephen, who died in 1299, is buried in Penshurst Church. It was in 1552 that it passed into the hands of the Sidneys, who have held it ever since. The present owner, Lord de Lisle and Dudley is particularly generous in allowing visitors to see the many historic treasures of his famous home.

The charm of the church, which stands close by the house, is enhanced by unusually picturesque timbered Tudor cottages that border the south side of the churchyard, a wide opening beneath the centre one forming a sort of lych-gate. This church which has a Perpendicular tower was originally Norman, but the whole church was entirely restored by Gilbert Scott. In the Sidney Chapel largely rebuilt in the early Georgian period, are monu-ments to many of the Sidney family, though not to Sir Philip, who was buried in St. Paul's. The remains of Algernon Sidney, executed in 1683, were, however, interred in the Sidney vault.

In addition to the genuine Tudor cottages there are several half-timbered ones, and a notable forge with a large horse-shoe shaped porch, which look old but are in point of fact mid-Victorian (28), the cottages being the work of George Devey, a pioneer architect in the revival of good domestic architecture, whose work is all too little known.

South again, right on the Sussex border, placed on the side of a wooded hill, stands Groombridge, a particularly delightful place, its timbered tile-hung and weather-boarded cottages all grouped round a triangular sloping green, intersected with little cobbled paths. The little Stuart brick church contains windows commemorating Sir Richard Waller and a marble table to W. C. Oswell, who was with Livingstone when he first saw the waters of the Zambesi.

It was to Groombridge Place that Sir Richard Waller brought his royal prisoner of Orleans from the fields of Agincourt, and found him so profitable a hostage that he was able to rebuild his house. The present Groombridge Place is over 200 years later than this, yet it is getting on for 300 years from our time, and makes one of the pleasantest pictures of a later Stuart house to be found anywhere. It is circled by a moat, and under hipped roofs the end projecting wings are connected by an entrance colonnade. The garden layout, preserving its original form, is modest, yet particularly charming, with terraces on different levels, and little clear running streams, and when I was there years ago, fine peacocks strutted over the lawns. One of the larger rooms is beautifully wood-panelled, and its ceiling has a great modelled wreath of high relief flowers and fruit, typical of its fine period.

The road from Groombridge to Tunbridge Wells is of special interest by reason of the eerie-shaped sandstone rocks worn by wind and rain (29) into the very forms of the iguanodons which used to roam on the banks of the prehistoric river that once swept over this land. And as we come over Rusthall Common to Mount Ephraim we look down over the town common to the famous inland spa.

Drawn by W. Curtis Green, R.A.

GROOMBRIDGE PLACE

VI

TUNBRIDGE WELLS TO ROMNEY MARSH

ROYAL Tunbridge Wells, so difficult of access in Walpole's day, owes its popularity as a spa to the discovery in 1606 by Lord North of its health-giving chalybeate springs, and to the proximity of Eridge Castle, the home of Lord Abergavenny who helped to make it fashionable. In 1630 Charles I's Queen came to the town for her health, but had to camp on the magnificent common, the town's supreme asset. Later Charles II's Queen often visited it and in the following century it became chief rival to Bath.

The Pantiles, with their avenue of lime trees and colonnade of old antique shops, still retain something of the atmosphere of their first great patrons, Beau Nash with his coach and six greys, Doctor Johnson, Lord Chesterfield, Pitt, Garrick, Richardson, Goldsmith and the Duchess of Kingston. There were baths and promenades and fountains and terraces and aristocratic villas, together with the many springs whose waters were the first cause of the town's fame. Just in the north end of the Pantiles (a pantile is a curved roofing-tile, but there are none there now) stands a sober little red brick Restoration church dedicated to King Charles the Martyr, where Queen Victoria's seat is still shown. It has a modelled plaster ceiling with impressive high-relief circular wreaths.

But Tunbridge Wells remains more in the memory by virtue of its scenic beauty than for its historic interest or architectural character, for it stands high and is set above and below a fine huge gorse-clad common with woodland glades and vast sandstone rocks, from which we look right over the Southern weald and the forest of Ashdown.

The county boundary, the famous Kent Ditch immortalised by Hilaire Belloc in *The Four Men*, lies away to the south-east. And the country, though far less well-known than that just on the other side of the border, is full of interest as well as of particular scenic attraction; if unspectacular it is well wooded and undulating, and as we shall see, thoroughly countrified and unspoilt.

First comes Lamberhurst on the Sussex border with its twin interests of Bayham Abbey and Scotney Castle. The village itself on the Hastings road is a pleasant place of excellent tile-hung, weatherboarded and plastered cottages sloping up from the little Teise, whose floods used to cut the Hastings coach traffic till the bridge came in 1717. The church is placed well away from the village in a retired spot; it is largely fourteenth century with a fifteenth century tower (32), original roofs and a splendidly carved Jacobean pulpit, the finest in the county (31). An active

centre of iron-smelting, the railings of St. Paul's were cast at
Furnace Mill Pond; a portion of them was transhipped to Canada
but wrecked on the way; some, salvaged at great expense, are now
in a Toronto Park. Some specimens of these railings are also in
the Lewes Musem.

The ruins of Bayham Abbey, actually just in Sussex, consist
mostly of walls, which show the long narrow Premonstratensian
nave and short East end. It is the attractive situation by the river
among trees and smooth lawns that really gives them their chief
appeal. Lord Camden's seat across the stream is a modern Tudor
house by Brandon. Scotney Castle has an equally fine situation,
with its one surviving machicolated Edwardian tower rising from
a moat and approached by an old bridge. It is companioned by
part of a Tudor house and the ruins of an unfinished seventeenth
century mansion. In a secret hiding place the Catholic Darells
successfully hid the Jesuit Father John Blount for several days in
1598. Here also the modern residence is a neo-Tudor building
standing apart; it was designed by Salvin.

This stretch of country between Tunbridge Wells and Cranbrook and the Sussex border, smiling, well cultivated and thickly
wooded, is perhaps the most attractive of all the Kentish Weald.
It is separated from the equally fine northern sandy Forest Ridge
round Sevenoaks by a very low-lying green valley—one of those
curious long corridors which are not traversed by the course of a
single river,—here the arrow-straight rail line from Redhill to
Ashford crosses the Eden, the Medway, the Teise, the Boult and
the Great Stour. This undulating well-wooded tract is really an
eastward but contrasting continuation of the heathland of Ashdown Forest; it is far more farm-tamed into pleasant fertility with
its hopfields and orchards. There is no sharp-cut escarpment like
the chalk downs a few miles north,—a welter of little hills tangled
all around, giving a surprising effect of relief, though only an
occasional patch is over 400 ft.; from such a high point as Goudhurst the view seems infinite in extent and unbounded in richness (4, 33). Man's contribution, also, of buildings is, save for the
staring nastiness of modern cottage or horror of Victorian church,
well knit and gracious in its design and craftsmanship. It is a joy
and delight on all counts to drive from anywhere round Goudhurst to Rye,—there used to be an excellent bus service,—and see
how the hills gradually die down, though still shaggy with woods,
till they yield to the coastal marshes beyond the flat green of the
Rother Valley.

Goudhurst is as attractive for its excellent buildings as for its
grand situation; weatherboarded or hung with deep red tiles (4),
they climb the steep slope to the church or cluster round a small
green. Their excellent craftsmanship may be due to the wool
stapling business, of which a little lingered to the early nineteenth
century. Admirers of Frank Kendon's charming autobiography

The Small Years will hardly need the reminder that Goudhurst is
the place there so intimately revealed, and the scene of G. P. R.
James's *The Smugglers* is laid here; it is founded on the deeds of an
authentic band headed by one Radford. Here also Cobbett was
baulked of his wish to hear the Dean of Rochester and disappointed with the parson's Ersatz sermon. The church with its
stumpy lightning-struck tower is full of noteworthy monuments,—
earliest are brasses to Bedgeburys and Colepepers who acquired
the Bedgebury Estate. The 40 Colepeper monuments include one
to Alexander (1537) with 12 child effigies and another to Thomas
(1558) with 11 sons, 5 daughters and 2 infants. But the 1642
Campion tomb is outstanding. Below is the effective early Georgian
house of Finchcocks, with its side wings and pleasant simple
panelled interiors.

The Bedgebury Estate comprises an extensive forest which is a
prominent feature of easterly views from Goudhurst. The house
is now occupied by a girls' School; after many vicissitudes it was
recast in the form of a French château by a member of the Beres-
ford Hope family, and filled with historic treasures and Victorian
appointments on the most splendiferous scale. The grounds are, or
were, elaborate and magnificent; the rhododendrons are a splendid
sight when flowering.

Brenchley stands in fine wooded hilly country and has a number
of good timber houses in the village and surrounding country,
notably the Old Palace (34), once a single dwelling but now
divided. A clump of tall "umbrella" trees on a 350 ft. hill forms
an outstanding landmark. From the square the fine transeptal
thirteenth–fifteenth century church is approached by a yew
avenue, for the clipping of which a quart of beer per head was
once paid. There is a rare celure or canopy over the surviving part
of the Renaissance screen, of 1536 date.

Horsmonden also has memories of cloth-making and iron-
founding, supplying cannon balls and ordnance in the Restoration; later came the smugglers and highwaymen hanging in
chains. The village is pleasantly placed on a height and its old
houses surround a square green. The church as at Lamberhurst
stands away by itself; it has a fine fourteenth century brass in
mass vestments to one of the Grovehurst family, who died out
from the manor of that name in the time of Richard II. A screen
bears a Latin inscription bidding prayers for the good estate of one
Alice Campion. In the churchyard is a many-limbed walnut tree,
supported on a number of trucks. On a height near the rectory is
a glum-looking tower put up in 1858 by a former parson, Sir
William Smith Marriot, to the memory of Sir Walter Scott, and
containing a collection of his works. Scott has his abiding place in
literature, but no one would feel impelled to erect a tribute of
that kind now.

South of Bedgebury lies Hawkhurst, which to a Sussex man is

foreign country. Whenever I take the bus that runs from Brighton to Hawkhurst, after we leave Burwash with all its memories of Kipling and Puck of Pook's Hill I feel a sea-change come over me. We dip into a bottom, cross the Kent Ditch and I feel much more in a strange land than I do when I cross the border into Wales or Scotland. What is there about Hawkhurst that is different from these other "hursts", Ticehurst, Wadhurst, and the rest that lie within the confine of "seely" Sussex? There are the same red roofs. The wooden houses are white, and that is a difference. But the difference is atmospheric rather than scenic, though the presence of oast-houses betrays the proximity of hop fields, which don't rightly belong to Sussex.

It is the people. They are completely different. I often wonder whether the Kentish sojourner finds us in Sussex as strange as we find him. Anyway Hawkhurst is to me unmistakably Kent. It is certainly picturesque with its tall well proportioned fifteenth century church tower standing 75 ft. high among great chestnut trees. There is a memorial window to Sir John Herschel, the son of Sir William, the astronomer, who watched the stars for 30 years and died at his house Collingwood in 1871; he is buried near Newton in Westminster Abbey.

Nobody in his senses would visit Hawkhurst without going to Bodiam Castle, which is just to the south and over the Sussex border (35). Bodiam, bequeathed to the National Trust by the late Lord Curzon, is the mediaeval castle of our dreams, rising four-square and perfect above a wide moat with walls that are over forty, and towers over sixty feet high, with portcullis and machicolate great gate, under which we walk to grass courts past the great hall, kitchen, and lady's bower. The castle was built in 1386 and surprisingly has no history whatever. But in beauty it is comparable with Carnarvon, though of course very much smaller and less imposing. It is very difficult to believe that it is real, so perfect is it in every fourteenth century detail.

Standing high in a hollow between two hills is Cranbrook, though the principal Wealden market town a quiet enough little place, yet it was once a busy centre of the clothing industry, which was started by Edward III's settlement of Flemish weavers. A number of the old gabled weavers' houses remain, and some seats round about were once factories. It is said that Queen Elizabeth walked the whole mile to Coursthorne Manor on a carpet of broadcloth locally woven. The weatherboarded houses are dominated by a splendid windmill built in 1814. The church of St. Dunstan is of all periods, but principally spacious light Perpendicular; there is a complete window of fourteenth century glass in the North aisle, and monuments to the Robertses, who for centuries inhabited the moated manor of Glassenbury, where the family still dwell, though the house was modernised by Salvin in 1868. The church contains a large genealogical Roberts monument, and the helm, surcoat, gloves and spurs of one of the family. The barred Chamber over the south porch is still called Bloody Baker's prison, recalling Chancellor Sir John Baker's savage persecution of the local anabaptists. There is another reminder of Baptist feeling in the surprising baptistery built for total immersion in 1720 by the remarkable vicar John Johnson. Cranbrook is unusually rich in worthies,—Phineas Fletcher, poet of "the Purple Island", Sidney Dobell, poet, Douglas Jerrold, who was brought up at Willersley Green,—where there is a most adorable old house, —and has left a charming impression of the locality in his *Chronicles of Clovernook* and several artists. There is a grammar school of Elizabethan foundation, and a brick hall built to give work to the unemployed after the Napoleonic wars. The overseers of Cranbrook hired a farm which they called Idle Men's Farm, which paid so well that they were able to give a new clock to the church, and built this vestry hall, now used as the County Court.

But Cranbrook to me summons up yet another worthy, one Booth, a native who went out to Detroit, made a fortune out of newspapers and founded a magnificent school which is called Cranbrook, where I have seen boys and girls more splendidly housed than in any other school that I have ever visited.

Sissinghurst, on the outskirt of Cranbrook, has some fine old weatherboarded houses, a mill, an 1838 church, and a castle built by "Bloody Baker" which, after housing several succeeding generations fell on evil days and was used to keep Napoleonic prisoners of war and then as a poorhouse. The old gateway and imposing central red brick Tudor tower survived, however (36), and the place has recently been rescued from almost unimaginable weed-grown decrepitude by the authoress Vita Sackville-West and her husband Harold Nicolson (36).

Biddenden is a remarkably attractive village, once a centre of cloth weaving; one seven gabled half-timber building is known as the Cloth Hall, and some buildings still have or once had communicating attics, probably in connection with weaving. There is no need to describe its almost ultra-perfect street of old half-timber houses, as it is here illustrated and should be seen for itself. On both sides of the street is a 15 ft. wide crazy paving of slabs of Bethersden marble. But the place is most famed for its story of the two maids Eliza and Mary Chalkhurst or Chulkhurst; this is well known, but it may perhaps be permissible to summarise it here— they were a pair of Siamese twins joined at shoulders and hips. They lived for 34 years, till on the death of one the other refused to be severed and followed her in six hours. They bequeathed land for an Easter distribution to the poor and small cakes stamped with the maids' images are distributed to visitors and attract huge crowds. Hasted, Kent's star historian, throws doubt on the whole affair, but there is little doubt of its historical foundation, though the sixteenth century seems a more likely date than the

27   THE GREAT HALL, PENSHURST PLACE, KENT

28   COTTAGES IN THE OLD STYLE, 1851, BY THE ARCHITECT GEORGE
DEVEY IN PENSHURST VILLAGE, KENT

30 FURNACE POND, HORSMONDEN, KENT

29 THE HIGH ROCKS, NEAR TUNBRIDGE WELLS

Drawn by Sydney R. Jones

BIDDENDEN VILLAGE STREET, KENT

twelfth, as sometimes stated. The church is of good thirteenth–fifteenth century work and has a Jacobean pulpit. But it is noteworthy for its series of post-Reformation brasses, of a set of people remarkably given to marriage and children,—8 brasses commemorate 8 husbands (and one second), 13 wives and 45 children.

Benenden is a large pleasant village on high ground, with the remnant of an extensive forest to the north, and a green in which many notable cricket matches have been played; the oft-preferred claim that Lord Cranbrook's Hemstead Park is the highest point of all the Kentish Weald seems strange, though it all depends on the definition of the area in question; it has now come to the fore as a girls' school.

Rolvenden, the next of the dozen or score of "den" villages, is strikingly placed on high ground, and stands up well as you come to it from Tenterden. Nevertheless it is between the Hexden and New Mills Channels of the Rother valley; a mediaeval boat with human remains has come to light, as well as a fine Roman bronze vase. The street of old houses with green margins curves away pleasantly from the church, which has two remarkable squires' pews.

Facing across to Rolvenden is the almost idyllic unspoilt village of Sandhurst, on a lower odd scrap of ridge thrust out from Hawkhurst between the Hexden Channel and the Rother or Kent Ditch. The church has a sturdy austere tower with little penthouse aisles, and, uncommon for Kent, a clerestory, which is Early English and seems to have been underpinned on to a later arcade. Among some old stained glass is the figure of an armed knight.

G

Below the end of the little spur is Newenden, down by the Rother, navigable for barges, which separates Kent and Sussex. The three-arched bridge was built jointly by the two counties in 1700, and in the same year the church was bereft of chancel and tower, of which the stones were sold. But though the little nave looks truncated it contains a remarkable Norman font, richly carved with dragon monsters.

In the opposite or north-easterly direction from Rolvenden is Tenterden, largest and most important of the "dens"; in the district called "The Seven Hundreds" on an abrupt knoll overlooking the Rother levels. The main street is very broad, with green margins and planted with trees; its houses form a pleasant architectural patchwork of timber, tilehanging, weatherboarding and plaster. But the outstanding feature is the tall pinnacled tower with a double western entrance—"Tenterden steeple", from which there is a magnificent view of a wide stretch of undulating and marshy country dotted with church towers. Till recently it retained its iron beacon cresset, possibly used as an Armada warning. It has been traditionally and malignantly assigned to be the cause of the Goodwin Sands, and Latimer has left in a sermon a gossipy account of the enquiry held by Sir Thomas More, in which the oldest inhabitant declared the tower to be also responsible for the silting of Sandwich harbour. Among many interesting houses scattered around we may mention pleasant Westwell, a foursquare varied-brick Queen Anne building erected by James Blacknine in 1711, with original garden layout.

We are now on the threshold of Romney Marsh, and Walland Marsh, but there is first the ridge of the Isle of Oxney reached through Small Hythe, once a port but now a tollgate, with its little Tudor chapel and Ellen Terry's cottage. On the ridge stands Wittersham, where the church has a tall well-proportioned tower, Geometrical reticulated tracery and a finely carved late mediaeval lectern. On the way to Stone and Appledore, at The Stocks on the highest point of the ridge, is a delightful group of a mill, oast-houses and a lovely timber cottage.

At the pleasant village of Appledore with its wide street, we enter a new enchanted land. Roman legions in one age built banks here to keep the sea from trespassing further, and in another sappers dug a canal to flood the flat lands against invasion. The stumpy-towered church is a Norman building transformed; it was burnt in a French raid in the fourteenth century, just as the place was sacked by the Danes 500 years earlier. It has fine screens, and a tomb to Master Philip Chute, Henry VIII's standard bearer at Boulogne. At Harne Place, now a farm, is a beautiful fifteenth century domestic chapel with crypt and excellent tracery.

We will explore Romney Marsh itself in the next chapter.

32 LAMBERHURST CHURCH, KENT

31 THE JACOBEAN PULPIT AND STALLS, LAMBERHURST

33   THE SOUTH-EASTERLY VIEW FROM THE CHURCH TOWER, GOUDHURST

VII

ROMNEY MARSH TO CANTERBURY
AND DOVER

THERE is mystery and enchantment at all seasons of the year in the low-lying flat unhedged green fields of Romney Marsh, with the long water-dykes separating great flocks of the famous sheep, which have gone from here all over the world to add to the glory of English wool and English mutton (39). Farms are few and villages practically non-existent, but far over the vast plain you can see here and there a tower or a spire and a few trees protecting and hiding a marshland hamlet, or a great solitary farm and its barns.

The marshes, which are divided into Walland Marsh, Denge Marsh and Romney Marsh, occupy over 45,000 acres of rich alluvial land reclaimed by the Romans from the sea. Practically deserted now, except by sheep and the birds, they were well populated when the vast forest of Anderida was often impenetrable and tenanted by wild beasts. The Romans farmed it extensively and one of their potteries has been discovered at Dymchurch, where they built the great wall, as well as the Rhee Wall that runs from Appledore to Romney, which is so named after Rome, and marks the old course of the Rother.

I have always come to the marshes from the west by way of Rye, and there is little to be said in favour of the coast near or at Dungeness; it is littered with unsightly shacks and to be avoided. But Lydd is unexpectedly lovely. Its fifteenth century church tower rises 150 ft. above the flats and can be seen for miles both from sea and land. It was built when Cardinal Wolsey was rector, and stands among trees amid lichen-covered roofs that make one forget that Lydd is world famous for lyddite. The fine spacious church, which is 200 ft. long, still retains some of its Saxon walls and has an Early English nave arcade of seven bays, a noble kingpost roof, a late mediaeval screen and memorials to Sir Walter Merril, John Thomas, 1429, and Thomas Godfrey, a man who achieved the record of being thirty-four times mayor.

New Romney is of course not new any longer. It was at its zenith in 1287 when, according to Defoe, it had five parish churches, a priory and a hospital. Till somewhere about 1360 ships could come close enough to cast anchor in one of the churchyards. Indeed it was a Cinque Port, but now it is a mile and a half from the coast.

Some idea of its past glory can be gleaned from its fine church, which has a tower 100 ft. high and 32 ft. square, built in five stages, all Norman except the top. The floor of the church is below the general surrounding level, which has gradually silted up round it.

The church itself is partly Norman and partly Decorated, and the nave piers are alternately cylindrical and octagonal. The mayor is still elected within this church, the jurats assembling round the sixteenth century table tomb of Richard Stuppenye.

Old Romney, which lies two and a half miles west of New Romney, had dwindled to a hamlet as far back as 1377, when its population was much what it is today. The thirteenth century church of St. Clement has a picturesque shingled spire surmounting a small low grey tower (41). It contains high square box pews with seats on all four sides, the remains of an old coloured screen, fine tie beams and an old world gallery. In the churchyard there is one solitary ancient yew.

There are very few straight roads across the marshes, but two of them meet at Brenzett, which has some Norman work in its church (dedicated to St. Eanswith of Folkestone), a shingled spire on a small wooden tower, and is the burial place of a sixteenth century Oxford Professor, Thomas Becon, and of the Fogge family. Close by is Ivychurch, where St. Martin's Church has a tall turreted tower, and a hexagonal beacon turret, a conspicuous landmark, and is decorated with some fine Perpendicular stalls, but is rather derelict.

Some distance over the flat lands near the railway stands the marshland church of Fairfield, islanded, solitary and treeless at the end of a long grass causeway raised above the marsh, once accessible only by boat or horseback (40). It has a steep-pitched roof, coming down to the low walls, a squat wooden turret with three recast fourteenth century bells, walls of brick, and an interior almost wholly of timber, with a three decker pulpit and half a dozen box pews. Services are held but rarely, and it is more frequented by birds than men. Not far off is Brookland, where the fourteenth century church has a fine Norman lead font (9) with panels of fieldwork through the seasons and a curious diminishing-stage wooden belfry leaning detached in the churchyard; it has been suggested that Rhenish, or alternatively, Norwegian influence had a hand in its design (38). Its character and position give rise to several lively local stories, chiefly concerned with the doubtful virginity of marriage applicants. Its lonely inaccessibility has been referred to by Kipling in some moving lines of verse.

Most of us remember Dymchurch, partly through Kipling's story in *Puck of Pook's Hill* and partly by reason of John Davidson's haunting verses :—

> As I went down to Dymchurch wall
> I heard the South sing o'er the land:
> I saw the yellow sunlight fall
> On knolls where Norman churches stand.

It was the Romans who saved Dymchurch from the sea, which in their day ran up to the hills of Lympne and Appledore. They are by tradition reputed to have built the famous wall which runs 20 ft. high for four miles, wide enough to drive along, a stout bulwark without whose protection the marshland would be utterly inundated by the sea. There is a most unusual and picturesque walk to be had along the tree-fringed banks of the military canal below Hythe, on reaching which we change again quite suddenly from a deserted world of green fields to a place of seaside visitors, promenades and bathers.

Hythe, once a Cinque Port, still retains its old-time narrow streets and passages, but the port has long been silted up, and the town stands high and dry up on the hillside far away from the beach.

The old cruciform parish church is of unusual interest, the walls of the nave dating from about 1100. The chancel, built about 1220, is a magnificent example of Early English architecture. The noble Tower with its pyramidal stone capping is of the same period. Over the fine thirteenth century south porch is a priest's chamber, used up to 1734 as a council room. Municipal documents of great antiquity, including the charters of Edward I and III, are still housed in it. Beneath the chancel is an exceptionally fine crypt, entered by a beautiful doorway which leads into a lofty groined passage which has been turned into an ossuary, probably for skeletons of mediaeval date. Some purists deplore it, but its tourist popularity is enormous.

Sandgate is memorable chiefly for the eyesore of Shorncliffe Camp, and the fact that Sir John Moore fortified it strongly against the possibility of Napoleonic invasion. And so we come to Folkestone, standing magnificently above the chalk cliffs that stand as sentinels guarding the narrow straits.

Unlike a number of seaside resorts, Folkestone has an atmosphere that is all its own, a sort of crystal glitter, and countryside beauty. Much of its charm is of course due to those winding steep walks along and up and down the white cliffs. It is also largely due to the fact that it has wisely kept so much of its old town intact. William Harvey's fine statue reminds us that this was the birthplace of the discoverer of the circulation of the blood; he is also commemorated by the west window in the church subscribed for by 3,000 doctors.

In the church lie the remains of the Saxon princess, St. Eanswythe, who founded an abbey that has been overwhelmed by the sea. The thirteenth century nave of the church was blown down in 1702, but the contemporary chancel stands with its glorious brass gates. There are also traces of the Roman occupation, but perhaps the main glory of Folkestone lies in the high downs that stand above it to the north, which provide a grand walk all along their tops to Dover and Canterbury.

Just east of Folkestone is the famous Warren, where a series of landslides have converted a wilderness and jungle into a labyrinthine way of footpaths among trees that lead us past Shakespeare's cliff to Dover, one of the greatest heroic ports in the world. Through all our history Dover has been our sentinel and outpost, the port from which generations of warriors have gone forth to give battle to preserve their island home.

It is entirely fitting that on these heights, nearly five hundred feet above the sea, stands the oldest building in our island, the Roman pharos or lighthouse, cheek by jowl with the mediaeval church, a Saxon tower and the strongest of Norman castles, with a keep 91 ft. high and a well 400 ft. deep. Through its tunnel Penchester brought 400 men to capture the port in 1216.

Here too stands the memorial to Blériot, the first man ever to fly the Channel, a landmark of 1909, and the obelisk to the Dover Patrol, with the piers and breakwaters of the mighty harbour running for a long distance far below. In the town itself you can still see the walls of the priory set up by Hubert de Burgh, and in the Town Hall (de Burgh's Maison Dieu) the whole history of Dover is set out in a set of eight modern stained glass windows, the work of Sir Edward Poynter. Next to the Town Hall is the old Cloth Hall, where hangs the old town bell of Antwerp. There are two old churches much altered, and a famous Public School, Dover College.

Travellers today are in so great a hurry either to leave the country, or to get back to London, that they miss altogether the delights of our ancestors, who leisurely walked the Pilgrims' Way, or in a later age travelled by coach along the Dover Road, a journey immortalised by Charles Dickens. The road is straight and runs along the crest of the hills, while the Pilgrims' Way meanders, now a green track, now a lane, and now a road, among the hamlets and villages of a lost world.

So let us turn our back on France and make a zig-zag way among these smooth chalk downs and wooded dells north-westwards towards the cradle of Christianity. At Temple Ewell we have reminders of the Knights Templars, and at Swingfield, a lonely upland outpost, on a common with a thirteenth century church, is the preceptory of the Knights Hospitallers, now a farm called St. John's, where King John is supposed to have surrendered his crown, erroneously, however, for it took place in the Templars church, Dover.

We climb over Lydden Hill to Denton, a richly wooded village with the great house of Denton Court standing among yews in a park of 180 acres where the poet Gray used to wander. This is the country of *The Ingoldsby Legends*, for Richard Barham lived at Tappington Farm, where is a remarkably fine staircase.

We are now on the long stretch of Barham Downs, with the fine mid-seventeenth century brick many gabled mansion of Broome Park, once the house of Lord Kitchener, standing superbly among the woods. Broome Park was built in 1638 for

34 BRENCHLEY VILLAGE, KENT, WITH THE OLD PALACE ON THE RIGHT

35 BODIAM CASTLE

36 SISSINGHURST CASTLE, NEAR CRANBROOK, WITH "BLOODY BAKER'S"
TOWER

Sir Basil Dixwell, who signed the death warrant of Charles I, and then passed to the Oxendens, one of whom, a murdered wife, still haunts it. King Edward VII tried to buy it before he bought Sandringham, and when Kitchener acquired it, he spent much time in altering it and pulling it about, but never lived to pass a single night in it. It is an extensive and extremely picturesque country house, with a multitude of tall rectangular windows, ornate Dutch gables, dormer windows and tall stacks of chimneys. After functioning for a spell as a country hotel it is at the time of writing in military occupation.

All the country round Barham Downs is magnificent, for there are vast open fields with happy-looking prosperous farms, each with its dozen or so cowl-topped oast houses, and field paths running in all directions. Southward, the Folkestone line runs through a charming deep wide wooded valley to Elham and Lyminge, both places of considerable charm.

Elham has a spacious square with fine sixteenth century rows, of which the timbering has recently been sympathetically uncovered (42), and a large imposing church that has early square piers, and a good fourteenth century yew chest. There is a fine library in the vestry, with rare tracts of the Civil War. The adjoining Tudor house has fine exterior and interior carved work.

Lyminge is mainly memorable for the church built by St. Ethelburga of Northumbria, who founded a nunnery here and ultimately died at this place. There are interesting but fragmentary remains of her building. There is a bridle track on the way to Canterbury that is still known as Queen Ethelburga's Grove, and a Queen's Well that also commemorates her. The Saxon work was roughly built by St. Dunstan when he transferred the Queen's remains to Canterbury. Nearby on the hills to the east lies the famous Roman road of Stone Street, which runs straight as an arrow from Canterbury almost to Hythe without passing through a single village.

One of the best walks I ever took was on the exteme western edge of this last breast of the North Downs, along the tops above Wye to Stowting. You wind your way in and out along the edge of a very high plateau with commons, woodlands, fields and farms compactly hidden among the folds of the hillside. In the valley, almost encircled by the hills, is Stowting with a church beautifully situated in an almost deserted high banked lane. Close by is Monks Horton with a fine park and priory that once belonged to Walter Mantell who said at his execution "Surely, you will let a dying Kentish man breathe the air of his beloved county."

A later owner was Lord Rokeby, known to readers of *The Ingoldsby Legends* as the man who used to tuck his beard between his legs.

It is time to get back to Barham Downs with the high-standing magnificent white windmill and the beautiful village of Bishopsbourne, that is reached by way of an avenue of pines and beeches as you descend from Watling Street. It lies between two great parks, a group of church, village hall, vicarage, forge and stream. Bishopsbourne is mainly interesting because it was once the home of Joseph Conrad and Richard Hooker who was rector here for the last five years of his life. The Perpendicular church is of no particular interest.

Above Bishopsbourne, right on Watling Street, stands the long street of Bridge, with its windmill, shingled church spire, lichen-covered roofs of white cottages and remains of the great house of Bourne Park. Here an historic cricket match was played in 1773 between Kent and Surrey. In a hollow in the park called Old England's Hole Julius Caesar is said to have gained his first decisive victory on British soil.

But Bridge is overshadowed by its neighbour Patrixbourne which boasts a church which contains one of the finest examples of a Norman doorway tympanum in the country (45). It has a thirteenth century shingled spire among trees and half-timbered cottages, which are not as old as they look, are graced by the beauty of the little stream by their doors.

We are now in sight of the towers of Canterbury Cathedral (44). It is best reached by keeping along the Pilgrims' Way which is here an attractive path running through hopfields.

Drawn by J. Alfred Gotch

PORTION OF THE PARGETTING PATTERN
ON A HOUSE AT WIVENHOE (v. p. 131)

37   "PATTENDEN," GOUDHURST, A KENTISH YEOMAN'S HOME

38   BROOKLAND CHURCH, WALLAND MARSH, KENT, WITH ITS CURIOUS
DETACHED TIMBER BELFRY

VIII

CANTERBURY AND THE ISLE OF THANET

THE old cradle and centre of English Christianity has a new appeal since it is battle-scarred from the malicious spite of enemy air-savagery. In spite of damage to St. Augustine College and elsewhere its grace and charm are little marred.

Whichever way you come into Canterbury it is of course the exquisite central tower of the Cathedral, Bell Harry, that holds the eye most surely, rising as it does majestically above a host of famous buildings (44). We may well pause before the stout City Gate to recall how precarious is the continued life of some of our ancient monuments, for the circus manager Wombwell in 1859 very nearly prevailed upon the Corporation to have it removed to make room for the passage of his elephants; only by the mayor's casting vote was it preserved.

City walls were here before the Romans came to strengthen them by setting up 21 watching towers and seven gateways, of which only this one remains—the West gate, the work of Archbishop Sudbury (1374–81), beheaded by the London rabble on Tower Hill. Through this gate came the endless procession of pilgrims to the shrine of St. Thomas à Becket after Henry II walked barefoot to the crypt to be scourged for the infamous crime of the Archbishop's murder. In later years condemned prisoners spent their last nights in this gateway before going to the gallows. This west gate is surely one of the finest examples of its kind in the Kingdom. It was rebuilt in 1380, and the guard chamber on the archway used as the city gaol for nearly three hundred years; later the top part was converted into a museum.

The castle keep, the fifth largest in Great Britain, dates from the reign of Henry II, and has state rooms on the second and third floors and a great hall on the third. It has had a curious history, changing in the course of time from royal palace to prison, and pumping station to coal store; today it is a public show place.

The city wall with its turf banks and turrets and prehistoric Dane John, much altered through the centuries, stands close by, but the best part of the old walls are in Broad Street, where there still stand three small watch towers.

Before being tempted to enter the Cathedral, which is so full of interest as to make one overlook the other treasures of this rich city, you should pay a visit to St. Augustine's Abbey.

The Great Gate, which is entered from Lady Wootton's Green, was once a brewhouse, and the great Hall and Kitchen reclaimed from being used as a public-house just a hundred years ago, and adapted and reconstructed.

H

Some thirty years ago remarkable excavations were made so that you can now see the lower parts of the walls of the church of St. Pancras built by St. Augustine in 597, and some of the foundations of the abbey church begun by the saint and finished in 613.

Then comes the plan of the great Norman church in which the sacred relics of the saints were housed. The north wall had its windows filled up in Tudor times to make a tennis court.

The tombs in the south transept of the Saxon Kings and their wives, though not that of St. Augustine, may still be seen.

A little way out of the city, standing on a knoll by a windmill is the little church of St. Martin, generally accepted as the first place of Christian worship in England. It was here that St. Augustine and his followers met in 597, and you can still see Saxon workmanship mixed up with the Roman brick.

King Ethelbert is said to have been baptised in the Saxon font, which is of three tiers and has an ornamental rim. The north doorway is Norman and there is a particularly beautiful Norman piscina. There are also two fine sixteenth century brasses and a fine open roof.

Of Canterbury's other churches you should see the thirteenth century St. Dunstan's, where in the Roper vault lies the head of Sir Thomas More and the body of his favourite daughter Margaret, and St. Mildred's with its Saxon and Roman work. It was here that Izaak Walton married his first wife, Rachel Floud.

The picturesque Grey Friars house in Stour Street was once the home of the poet Richard Lovelace, and of the old Grey Friars on the banks of the river you can still see the thirteenth century flint refectory, once used as the Cloth Hall and later as a Unitarian Chapel, with its Guest House on the opposite bank. Of other ancient historic houses the outstanding are the group of timbered houses with Flemish gables known as the Canterbury Weavers which like so many other local buildings has changed its occupation more than once. This too was converted into an inn; it has now reverted to its original purpose of weaving.

Opposite the Weavers is Henry I's Eastbridge Hospital with a twelfth century hall. There also is an eleventh century Hospital of St. John the Baptist, also with its hall intact, the Poor Priests' hospital rebuilt in 1373, Maynard's Hospital and Jesus Hospital.

In St. Martin's Street was till it fell a recent victim to a senseless air raid the very ancient *Royal Fountain Hotel*, described by a German Ambassador in 1299 as the best in Canterbury. "The inns in England," he wrote "are the best in Europe; those of Canterbury the best in England, and the *Fountain* the best in Canterbury."

But it is on the Cathedral that visitors rightly concentrate their time, for there is the whole history of Christian England. First our eyes in peacetime are arrested by the dazzling display of stained glass, much of which dates back to Norman times. First in interest are probably the nine miracle windows that record the life of St. Thomas à Becket. One window shows what an amazingly rich shrine Becket's must have been. In spite of the destruction wrought in the time of Laud by "Blue Dick" (Richard Culmer), vicar in turn of five local churches, in "rattling down proud Becket's glassie bones" there is enough of this noble deep-coloured work (p. 62) to make the cathedral the greatest repository of early glass in the land, as York Minster and parish churches are collectively of the later work.

Next we may place the fine fifteenth century old screen with figures of the kings in the niches. Then come the little chapels round the choir, the finest of which is the shrine of Henry IV, but the most cherished is the Warriors' Chapel, not so much for the sake of Stephen Langton who lies here, as for the Roll of Honour Book of the Buffs. But the chapel is crowded with monuments of many dates and varying design, of interest for their design, as for the folk they commemorate; indeed the whole fabric is splendidly rich in sterling indigenous monumental art of more than five centuries; I recall one tomb which has the finely sculptured representation of a great ship. I find myself revisiting most often the superb tomb of the Black Prince, richly coloured, with his helmet, coat, shield, scabbard and gauntlets hanging overhead. A whole host of Archbishops lie here, but only one King, Henry IV. You are of course shown the exact spot where St. Thomas received his death wounds, and no one can fail to see how the stone of the steps has been worn away by generations of kneeling pilgrims.

It is impossible to do justice to the architecture of Canterbury Cathedral, but it should be realised that a nave of late English Perpendicular is, in the only instance in England, tacked on to a choir of Transitional design, largely French in type. Prior Chillenden rebuilt the nave in the late fourteenth century, and its slender piers and tall windows lead the eye upward to the rich stellar lierne vault. We can compare its lofty grace with our other great Perpendicular nave at Winchester, which represents the amazing transformation of a vast and massive Norman work, a piece of brilliant ingenuity only rivalled by Gloucester choir. The long choir here at Canterbury is a complete contrast; it is raised by many steps above the crypts and is comparatively dimly lit, has plain vaults, and its apsidal end, coupled columns and Corinthianesque capitals are reminiscent of a Cathedral across the Channel, particularly it is thought of Sens, from where the master-mason-designer William came. You must read for yourselves in Gervase the Monk's account of the fire, how he departed from the monks' wish to have their beloved Norman work replaced, of his tragic fall and how William the Englishman carried on the work. Under the main floor stands the 230 ft. long crypt where the descendants of the Huguenots still hold a service in French each Sunday. Here too is a lady chapel, and a small French chapel built by the Black Prince, with two Saxon columns from the vanished church of Reculver. The wooden chair of St. Augustine stands not in the Cathedral but in the museum. The stone chair in the Cathedral is only about 700 years old. Outside the Cathedral there is a magnificent Norman staircase in the Green Court, which leads up to a room where Christopher Marlowe and William Harvey attended school. The King's School, which uses these Norman steps, claims with some justification to be the oldest in England. The great gateway that leads to the Cathedral is difficult to appreciate owing to the fact that it is badly hemmed in among narrow if picturesque streets which are full of memories of Charles Dickens.

Drawn by Sydney R. Jones

THE TOWN HALL, FORDWICH, SHOWING PRESS-GANG DRUMS AND DUCKING CHAIR ON ROOF

Eastwards from Canterbury we run through the valley of the Stour, a wide flat marshland which is the haunt of birds and anglers. Fordwich, just over two miles north-east of Canterbury on the Stour, is a most peaceful and picturesque ancient hamlet, the resort of anglers and artists. It was in turn a Roman settlement, a Norman borough and a member of the Cinque Port of Sandwich. There is a place on the river called "The Thieves' Wall" where the prosecutor had to hold the condemned man under the water in the presence of the constable until he was dead.

The monks of St. Augustine's Abbey once possessed a quay here, and later the monks of Christ Church Priory established a rival one where they landed the Caen stone for the building of the Cathedral as well as corn, wine and oil for the builders.

There is a half-timbered Town Hall with stone and brick patch-work, restored in 1474, with a Council Chamber that has large tie beams in the roof, oak mullioned windows and panelling, the press-gang drums and a ducking chair (p. 56). In the church of St. Mary the Virgin, which has a tower with a tall shingled spire, there is some Saxon work, as well as Norman, Decorated windows, high square eighteenth century pews and a tomb with scale pattern top that was once the top of a Roman sarcophagus, with side sculpturing of intersecting arches on 19 Roman pillars. There is also a heart-shrine, one very good brass and a penitent's stool carved out of a tree trunk.

Izaak Walton talks of the "Fordidge" trout being "near the bigness of salmon". "In their best season they cut very white."

The neighbouring hamlet of Sturry stands pleasantly on the banks of the river with a narrow rising single arched bridge, and church with a fair fifteenth century tower and tall weather vane. It has a Norman chancel and nave and a fourteenth century timber porch, but otherwise it has been drastically restored.

Some distance south on the banks of the lesser Stour stands Wickhambreaux with a lime-shaded green and a church that has been too much restored. There is a pleasant view of this unpretending little church across the river, and the Flemish-looking post office has a chequer of flint and stone and twin stepped gables.

Some six miles west of Canterbury, standing at a junction of five ways, is the old market town of Wingham with old timbered houses, fine wide shady street and a spacious cruciform church on the corner of the green with fourteenth century tower surmounted by a green leaded spire, thirteenth century chancel and aisle and remains of an old wood screen, and collegiate stalls and fifteenth century nave windows. A sixteenth century wooden arcade runs between the nave and the south aisle.

Opposite the church is a picturesque row of old timbered houses, two of which are inns, the fifteenth century *Lion* and the *Dog*. The beauty of these houses and the spaciousness of the church are partly explained by the fact that Archbishop Peckham founded a college here. The remains of the Archbishop's manor house can still be seen as well as the prebendal houses.

Nearer Sandwich is the large and pleasant village of Ash, the fine central fifteenth century tower and leaded spire of the church of St. Nicholas standing up as a landmark for many miles. This church possesses many fine monuments, the oldest being the effigy of a knight of Edward II's reign, and one of the handsomest alabaster figures of a fourteenth century knight and lady. There are also many good brasses.

A network of lanes leads us to Barfreston or Barfreystone, which boasts an extremely lovely little church that is late Norman and built of Caen stone. It measures 43 ft. by 16¼ ft. Particularly impressive are a fine wheel window at the east end (46), the triple archways of the chancel and eight sundials on the south wall of the nave, six of them round the south doorway, which has a magnificently carved tympanum (50).

It is time now to make for the coast.

The nearest place of interest is Walmer, now a suburb of Deal. The castle built by Henry VIII for coast defence is the seat of the Lord Warden of the Cinque Ports. The Duke of Wellington lived here for 23 years and died in it.

Deal, now a holiday resort, also boasts a castle contemporary with that of Walmer, with six round bastions of stone, and a massive round tower with exceptionally thick walls. It is a place with a historical association, for here Richard I landed on his return from Palestine. At Deal Perkin Warbeck began his rebellion, and Prince Charles was routed when he sailed into the Downs in 1645.

The church of St. Leonard was built in the eleventh century and rebuilt in the seventeenth. The red brick tower with its octagonal lantern and vane-topped cupola is a very happy example of this period.

At Goodnestone we have memories of Jane Austen, who stayed at Rowling House with her brother and talks of its famous fair where a yearly distribution was made of gold paper and coloured persian. The thirteenth century church has a monument to the Royalist soldier Sir John Boys.

Nearby is Sandwich, once famous as the oldest of the Cinque Ports and England's foremost harbour, today mainly known for its golf course. Curfew still rings at 8 p.m. and a matins bell at 3 a.m. in this quaint old-world port of narrow irregular streets of Dutch-type houses, with some of the Tudor period.

It suffered heavily from Danish raids, and it was here that Canute and Hardicanute landed with their armies to overrun the countryside. It was twice burnt by the French in Henry VI's reign, and reached its heyday in Henry VII's time when it was the chief naval and military port in the country. Then came the silting up of the harbour and its ultimate decay. It became a Flemish town in 1582 when the Fleming refugees came to alter its architecture and in some degree its life. This war has again brought it refugees after 350 years, this time from Czechoslovakia.

St. Clement's church has a massive Norman central tower arcaded on all four sides and supported by 12 fine richly carved columns. There is a fifteenth century nave with a fine roof. St. Mary's church, said to have been built by the Danes in 1009 and frequently rebuilt, possesses a most unusual fifteenth century communion cup and an exquisite Tudor font.

St Peter's church, also rebuilt in parts, is Norman in origin, and among other interesting points has an old tie-beam and kingpost roof, fine tomb canopy and unusual crypt.

In a town particularly rich in old houses, the best are in Church Street and Stroud Street. The Old House or King's Lodging is two-gabled with a timbered top and bears the date 1534.

The Hospital of St. Bartholomew, a twelfth century foundation, has been converted into 16 small houses. The sixteenth century Guildhall possesses records going back to 1432. Manwood Court, built in 1563, was originally the Grammar School. The Fishergate with three storeys above a painted arch and portcullis grooves was built in the fourteenth century.

The very attractive Barbican with its bastions of chequered stone and flint dates from 1539, and the Flint House, now St. Peter's Rectory, has a fine oak stairway.

The town was enclosed in 1384 and the ramparts provide a considerable walk.

A mile and a half from Sandwich on a cliff above the wide green marshes rise the ramparts of Rutupiae or Richborough which under Roman rule became England's chief port, but now is left high and dry. Close inshore were the oyster-beds that supplied the supper tables of Imperial Rome. It was here that Carausius ruled as Emperor for ten years before he was murdered by his henchman Alectus. Later more Emperors were elected and murdered by the garrison, and in the end when Rome fell the ramparts crumbled and were left derelict. Now the imaginative mind is left to reconstruct its past glories from the relics in the museum, where we realise with something of a stab of surprise how civilised and comfortable were the inhabitants of this once famous Gibraltar of the North.

In Pegwell Bay over the wide Minster marshes you can still see the actual landing-place of the Saxons. The very names are significant—The Monks' Well, Bloody Point, Ebbstreet, St. Augustine's Well and Thunor's Leap. Thunor had murdered a royal princess to put Egbert on the throne, and over the grave a phosphorescent light glowed, which made Egbert confess, and as a penance he had to build a monastery to cover as large a territory as a hind would traverse in a single course. The hind let loose ran with amazing speed, and Thunor in attempting surreptitiously to head it back to sea found the earth open before him to swallow him up at Minster chalkpit. It was on this beach that Canute attempted to stay the waves. Some of the ruins of Minster Abbey still stand, and the church has good Norman arches.

We are now on the threshold of London's most popular holiday resorts, Ramsgate, Broadstairs and Margate, where the air is always dry, sweet, clear and invigorating; they also form a Mecca of England's best known preparatory schools. Ramsgate somehow contrives to keep a partly foreign, partly Regency air about it that is slightly reminiscent of Weymouth; this is also partly due to its fine harbour, while crowds usually so entirely swamp Margate that we are apt to forget Lamb's panegyric and Mrs.

Caudle's curtain lectures until we escape into the long dark church which is unusually rich in brasses. Everybody of course knows Margate Grotto with its 2,000 shells, but the real antiquities are the ruins of Salmestone Grange, the Draper almshouses, and the fourteenth century gateway to Garlynge, once the home of the Dandelyons, and later of C. J. Fox.

Westward along the coast stand the fine twin towers of Reculver, where Ethelbert ended his days and the parson 130 years ago rabidly destroyed nearly all the old historic Saxon church to build a nasty new vicarage at Hoath.

At Herne, however, still stands the church whose tower was described by Ruskin as one of the three perfect things in the world. This was the church of the martyr Ridley, whose chair can still be seen. There are good brasses, an ancient screen, fourteenth century font, and a monument to Charles Dickens's friend Samuel Weller May, a name now as imperishable as that of Pickwick. But it is before the flint tower that so excited Ruskin that we shall pause longest, to admire its vaulted roof and the way it rises in layers of brown stone and black flint above an avenue of horse chestnuts.

Drawn by Sydney R. Jones

READY FOR ACTION:
THE FORDWICH DUCKING STOOL
AT THE TOWN HALL

40   FAIRFIELD CHURCH ON ROMNEY MARSH

41   OLD ROMNEY CHURCH ON THE MARSH

43 AT ELHAM, KENT

42 A CORNER OF THE SQUARE, LENHAM, KENT

IX

MAIDSTONE TO CANTERBURY

MAIDSTONE, Kent's County town, is an excellent medley of old and new, full of character and much beauty, well set on the Medway with the long lines of the chalk downs stretching north, west and south-east.

It is commercially very busy in spite of the fact that it can scarcely any longer be termed a port. Barges of course still transfer pulp for the famous paper mills at Larkfield and other places along the tidal ways as well as cement and beer, and its river links up the two great routes from London to the coast.

Historically it has always been well in the picture since the Saxon first built a castle here, and it is especially noteworthy for being the centre of agitation leading to better conditions for the peasants. Both Wat Tyler's and Jack Cade's rebellions had their inception here.

In the fourteenth century the Franciscan friars established themselves in the town and a religious guild was founded in 1424. In spite of a strong Royalist sympathy in the Civil War Fairfax defeated the king's followers here, but in Defoe's time the town had recovered sufficiently to make him comment on its commercial prosperity.

Among the buildings the fine Perpendicular church of All Saints' with its 80 ft. high tower stands out pre-eminent for its long chancel and beautiful sedilia on the edge of the tomb of the first warden of the College, to which belonged the choir stalls. Among an enormous number of monuments is one of Sir Lawrence Washington, an ancestor of George Washington.

Close to the churchyard are the gateway tower, river tower, remains of cloisters and other relics of the Perpendicular Ecclesiastical College built in 1395–96.

The Archbishop's Palace, built of ragstone with a Jacobean front which backs on the Medway, has a panelled banqueting hall, and other interesting rooms. Also near the river is the Hall of the Brotherhood of Corpus Christi, dating from the early part of the fifteenth century.

Among other notable buildings are the vicarage, the Gothick Mill Farm-house, the Tudor "Stone House" with a plaster front and panelled hall, now used as the official residence of the Judges on assize, the birthplace (in Earl Street) of William Hazlitt, and Chillington House, built in 1562 which is now the museum, remarkable for its magnificent collection of prehistoric worked flints and Roman remains.

But perhaps the most striking feature that we see from Maidstone tower is the long line of the North Downs beckoning to us to take the Pilgrims' Way to Canterbury. But before we pick up that lonely green track there are features in the valley that we cannot afford to pass by unseen. First Loose, Otham and Leeds. Loose is the name both of the river and the village, a place of winding ways with narrow up and down paths and bye-lanes and a stream that keeps on disappearing underground and running under tiny bridges below the overhanging windows of medieval cottages. But Loose's great attraction is its exquisite Manor House, magnificently restored by Colonel Statham and now the property of the National Trust, a gem of Tudor front and seven stone fire-places as well as a Priest's hiding-place.

Otham is famous for the number of its fine smaller Tudor houses of Kentish yeoman type, Synyards with close timbering and a later dormer, Wardes similarly but slightly larger, the Tudor House of Gore Court standing in its own park, and Stoneacre, given to the National Trust by Mr. Aymer Vallance who restored to it its central hall. All these houses are fifteenth or even partly fourteenth century in date and each is in its own way distinctive.

Not far off is the large gabled Tudor half-timber house of Rumwood Court in Langley parish, and Sutton Valence village, set dramatically on the edge of the sandy escarpment with wide views over the Weald.

But the outstanding triumph of this part of Kent is Leeds Castle, one of the most complete Norman fortresses in the King-dom, greatly enlarged in Tudor times. It stands on an island surrounded by a wide moat that enormously enhances its majesty, in a park of 500 acres. It was here that Henry VIII made a home for Katharine and wooed Anne Boleyn. Here too in after years Anne's daughter Elizabeth was imprisoned, as well as in earlier days Richard II. In Cromwell's time it was the home of Fairfax, and still contains relics of its more famous inhabitants, the most touching being a pair of little pink shoes belonging to Anne Boleyn.

It is high time to start our journey along the Pilgrims' Way. The best starting point from Maidstone is Aylesford, that ford on the Medway where Hengist and Horsa fought their way into Britain. Just above on the hill-side stand three large monoliths covered with a roof stone known as Kit's Coty House, largest and most important of South-Eastern cromlechs. There are prehistoric stones all over the place here: White Horse Stone (now destroyed), the Countless Stones, and the great covered cromlech of Coldrum, a little way off near Allington.

The main interests of Aylesford are its six-arched fourteenth century bridge and the splendid monuments in the fifteenth century church to the Culpepers, who owned old Preston Hall for 600 years and to Sir John Banks of the Friary. This too was the birthplace of the Restoration poet Charles Sedley.

44   CANTERBURY CATHEDRAL FROM THE NORTH

46   THE EAST END, BARFRESTON CHURCH, KENT

45   THE NORMAN SOUTH DOORWAY, PATRIXBOURNE,

The green bridle path of the Pilgrims' Way runs along the sides of the chalk downs about one-third of the way up the slopes where they change from gentle to steep. Just below lies Detling with Tudor gateway, dovecot and fourteenth century four-desk oak lectern. Above on the hill-top lies a bare space from which you can see over the rich orchards and hop fields of the Medway Valley right across the green garden of Kent to the wooded hills of the Sussex border. The temptation, unless you love solitude and the quiet lane where only rabbits and hedgerow birds move in the stillness, is always to be climbing up to get a wider view, or lower to explore the chain of villages that are linked by the busy road below.

Two of these that you will probably not want to miss are Harrietsham and Lenham. At Harrietsham are Stede Court which boasts one of the oldest walnut trees in England, Lake Cottage with its Pilgrims' Pond, and a striking fourteenth century church tower, with some excellent close-spaced timbered houses.

Lenham has an ancient square with a row of limes, cobbled streets, timbered houses (42), a spacious Decorated mediaeval church with fine oak door, superbly carved Jacobean oak pulpit, stone armchair, ancient communion cup and specially attractive pews. This was the burial place of Mary Honywood, who dying at the age of 93 left 367 descendants. You can read all about her courage in visiting martyrs in Mary Tudor's reign in Foxe's *Book of Martyrs*.

The Pilgrims' Way west of Lenham changes from a lane to a green track and is therefore far more inviting to the walker. You are unlikely to meet anyone but tinkers, the blue smoke of whose encampment provides fair warning of their proximity. I am always hoping to meet another W. H. Davies or George Borrow among these nomads, but so far I have met no poet and only a few with even a smattering of true Romany.

It is well worth diverging from the track to tread the long street of Charing. Of the great Tudor palace of Charing Cranmer's banqueting hall, where Henry VIII dined on his way to the Field of the Cloth of Gold, still stands, though it is now a barn (47). You can judge of the original magnificence of the palace from the fact that it was big enough to entertain 5,000 of the King's and Queen's retinue in addition to their Royal selves. The church has a well-proportioned typical Kentish tower (47) rising above red-roofed houses with oriel windows, narrow twittens, a white windmill and very picturesque almshouses.

We are now approaching the wide breach in the North Downs made by the rich broad valley of the Stour, and the Pilgrims' Way now runs under thick avenues of trees into and through the great park of Eastwell, where the church stands picturesquely on the edge of a great lake (6).

Westwell, standing close to the great park of Eastwell, is a large village pleasantly ranged round a triangular green. Its church, which has a tower with shingled spire, has some interesting examples of Early English work and fine fourteenth century sedilia and piscina as well as a tall stone screen in the chancel arch.

Richard Barham, author of *The Ingoldsby Legends*, was curate here for three years. Eastwell lies entirely within the two thousand acre park of Lord Gerard, who lives in a vast modern pseudo Tudor mansion.

The Pilgrims' Way, which runs through the park, is marked by a succession of yew trees and changes from a deeply rutted overgrown track to a green open way over the grass. It leads past the few cottages that form the hamlet and within a few hundred yards of the 40 acre lake on the banks of which stands the church of St. Mary (6). This Perpendicular church, which is built of chalk, has one glorious stained glass window, a white figure of the Duke of Wellington's niece who died at 39, a finely carved chancel screen, the tombs of the Moyles, and of the last of the Plantagenets who lived and died as a labourer on the estate in Elizabeth's reign. He was discovered and looked after by Sir Thomas Moyle, Speaker of the House of Commons, who rebuilt Eastwell House in the middle of the sixteenth century.

Just outside the park wall is a very attractive triangular green, with the Pilgrims' Way cutting almost indiscernibly past an ancient church and an attractive farm-house before turning abruptly upwards over White Hill to be lost in the eerie forest of King's Wood above Godmersham, where all the trees lie as they have been blown by generations of hurricanes. But before we climb to this ghostly forest it is worth looking across to Wye, famous now for its agricultural college and race-course, but in earlier generations as the birthplace of Cardinal Kempe, the church builder, and Charles II's secret agent Mrs. Aphra Behn, the barber's daughter who became our first woman novelist and playwright. Before the Conquest it was a royal manor and was granted by the conqueror to Battle Abbey. The once big cruciform church with three aisles and three chancels was struck by lightning in 1571 and little of its ancient glory remains. Kempe built the fifteenth century college for priests, which later became a grammar school for boys and is now the agricultural college.

There is a glorious walk over the downs above Wye right along to the coast at Folkestone, which gives magnificent views all the way of the whole vale of Ashford and Romney Marsh. But our way lies towards Canterbury through this haunted wood, that Jane Austen must have walked if she walked at all, for she spent much of her time at the great early Georgian house of Godmersham Park, of many graceful interiors, with her brother, who had changed his name to Edward Knight.

Next to the church is Court Lodge Farm, once the thirteenth century summer home of the Priors of Canterbury. In the church

is a stone carving of Becket sitting on a cushioned seat, his right
hand raised in Benediction, sculptured not later than 1200. There
are Roman tiles here, and on the hill-top there is a long barrow
known as Juliberry's Grave, a prehistoric barrow set up about
2000 B.C., in which in after years the Roman General Julius
Laberius is reputed to have been buried. Through clearings of
the trees we get our first view of the splendid towers of Canterbury
faintly grey in the far distance below.

The Pilgrims' Way, which quite certainly originally ran through
Chilham Park, has been abruptly diverted to skirt it, so that the
deer which roam so freely in the King's Wood must pity their
domesticated rivals that are penned in these grounds. But when
we reach Chilham we forgive the castle owners for keeping their
deer in and the public out, for this village like Arundel preserves
a completely feudal atmosphere. Chilham is one of the most
attractive villages in Kent, standing as it does on a knoll, thickly
screened with trees. Round and near the ancient market square
is a wealth of picturesque timbered houses, notably Robin's
Croft with its vertical beams, built in the fifteenth century, and
the Post Office. High walls hide the park in which stands the
Norman Castle Keep, close to the modern mansion which was
built in the sixteenth century, it used to be said by Inigo Jones,
for Sir Dudley Digges. The cruciform church, built in 1534, is
enormous for the size of the place and contains some twelfth
century glass and among other monuments a group by Chantrey.

The usual way on to Canterbury lies in the valley along the
banks of the Stour, where we leave the solitude of our green Way
at Chartham.

Chartham is less lucky than Chilham, which is by-passed by the
main road, in that its street has to bear all the brunt of the Canterbury and coast-bound traffic.

On the south side of the village green is the cruciform aisleless
church of St. Mary which contains the fourth oldest brass in
England, commemorating Robert de Septvans who died in 1306.
Its chancel has windows of Kentish tracery design. There are
many burial grounds of Britons, Romans and Danes on the
neighbouring hills, the river Stour being here navigable when
the Danes sailed up beyond Ashford to destroy Great Chart. One
of the ancient inns here bears the name of *Artichoke*, which I do
not remember to have seen elsewhere.

At the neighbouring hamlet of Horton the church has been
converted into an oast-house, which again is something that I
have not seen anywhere else.

Alternatively and perhaps more wisely, those who have followed
the Pilgrims' Way so far, can end as they began by climbing up to
the old track that leads through the woods to Harbledown,
where they will be rewarded by resting where Chaucer's pilgrims
rested for the last time and heard their last story as they looked

down on the city of their desire. Here Lanfranc founded the leper hospital, now the almshouse, clustering round the Norman church, a place of great interest with its massive pillars and mediaeval benches. In the hall of the hospital are relics that vividly recall the rich mediaeval world through which Chaucer's merry pilgrims rode singing, gossiping and exchanging tales.

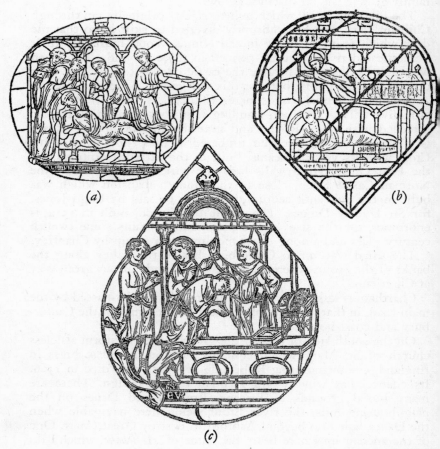

(a)   *(b)*

(c)

Drawn by N. H. J. Westlake

DETAIL OF EARLY CANTERBURY CATHEDRAL GLASS (*v. page* 50)

(*a*) From the Miracles at the Shrine of St. Thomas of Kent

(*b*) The Vision to Benedict, as related by himself, showing the Shrine in the Corona

(*c*) The cure of the Physician of Perigord at the Tomb of St. Thomas of Kent, in the Crypt, from a Window in Trinity Chapel

47 CHARING CHURCH AND THE RUINS OF THE ARCHBISHOP'S PALACE, KENT

49   SIR CLOUDESLEY SHOVEL'S FRIGATE AS THE VANE ON
          ROCHESTER GUILDHALL

48   STALL END CARVING, EAST BARMING, KENT, POS-
          SIBLY REPRESENTING THE VISIT OF CHRIST TO HADES

X

CANTERBURY TO SEVENOAKS *VIA* ROCHESTER AND SHEPPEY

I suppose no road in these islands has more romantic stories connected with it than the Dover Road or Watling Street, but the traffic is so heavy, and the road so altered today, that it is difficult to think of highwaymen, of Falstaff or Dickens at Gad's Hill, of French refugees in the Revolution or of stage coaches carrying fair ladies and brave men.

The road between Canterbury and Faversham is full of beauty, and Faversham itself which is an old market town has many interesting points.

A navigable creek capable of taking ships up to 200 tons connects it with the Swale, and in Defoe's time it was notorious for smugglers of brandy and French wine, and "owlers" who exported wool surreptitiously.

At the end of the eighteenth century the port was doing a brisk import and export trade, importing coal, timber and iron from Prussia, Norway and Sweden, and despatching wool, apples, pears, cherries and oysters. Today, there are gunpowder factories, brick and cement works, and a good trade is done in coal, timber and farm produce.

The church of St. Mary of Charity is a dignified cruciform building of almost cathedral-like proportions, with some original Decorated work in the chancel, several fine choir stalls, good brasses and a modern spire. In the Treasury, which has walls of rough chestnut timbers, were kept the treasures of 13 altars, guarded by watchmen who sat in the room above.

Among other notable buildings are the Old Guildhall in the market place, the ancient Grammar School, now used as the Masonic Hall, and the Gateway of King Stephen's Abbey.

There is a pleasant sleepy atmosphere about Faversham, partly induced by its sluggish creek. There is the smell that W. H. Hudson always regarded as peculiarly the smell of England, that of beer being brewed. There is down by the wharves the combined smell of mud and weeds and tar, which is also a typically English savour.

At Ospringe close by you see the curious sight of a river flowing between the houses, and carts and vans making their calls through water.

At Lynsted, just off Watling Street to the south, is a number of timber and plaster cottages of much attraction. Lynsted Park recalls the ancient house of Bedmangore, with links taking us back through the ancient family of Roper to the Plantagenets. Then

John Roper, first Lord Teynham, decided to build another house in 1599 connected with an avenue of limes. Lady Dacre added two wings, making up a hundred rooms and added six courtyards. Many of these rooms have been pulled down, but four of the courtyards remain, a black and white Elizabethan porch, and oak panelling and staircase. Lynsted, however, stands out equally for its series of medium sized timber houses, often of early date. The church, with its three long equal-width naves under separate gables, low sturdy tower and stumpy shingled spire of "timber-broach" type, is of outstandingly typical Kentish design; it has a cousinly resemblance to Westerham or New Romney, at the other ends of the county. None could occur anywhere else but in Kent, and all three bear witness to the strength and individuality of the county tradition. In the church there is the remarkable sculptured tomb of Christopher Roper, second Lord Teynham, the work of that strange little-known mystic genius, Epiphanius Evesham, whose work has been traced by Mrs. Katherine Esdaile. The lovely panel of the five mourning daughters, each in a strongly individual attitude, is quite unforgettable. Other monuments include the first Lord Teynham, a Cromwellian merchant, James Hugesson and Sir Drue Drury.

From Sittingbourne we look out over a desolate landscape of flats and marshes, cut by two estuaries and a number of creeks.

This is the Isle of Sheppey, a most strange mixture of the crudest bus-bungalows and shoddy shacks, factory chimneys and completely derelict marshlands. But at Minster-in-Sheppey there is a massive sturdy tower crowned with a diminishing stage louvre to remind us that there was a Saxon church here in the seventh century, burnt by the Danes and rebuilt by the Normans. There is still a Saxon arch and Roman tiles, with a brass of Sir Roger de Northwode 1320 and a fine tomb of Sir Robert Shurland, who died in 1272 and one of Sir Thomas Cheyne, once treasurer to Henry VIII, who was a dwarf and quite bald. Curiously enough he lies next to a giant, the seven feet tall Hugh, Lord de Badlemere, who was killed in the War of the Roses.

At Harty you get quite another picture of Sheppey life, for the bus only calls once a week, the school contains less than a score of children, and there is just an inn, a ferry, a solitary tree and a church. As far as the eye can see there is nothing but flat treeless, hedgeless dyke-patterned marshland, relieved here and there by the revolving sails of a water mill. You seem very near the sky and always very conscious of it. The church even in this remote outpost has its treasures. There is a good Norman arch, a fifteenth century screen, and a most unusual chest, with a panel of knights tilting, said to have been carved by German craftsmen in the fourteenth century. Lest, however, you should take Harty as typical of Sheppey, let me remind you that this island also contains Sheerness and Queenborough.

50   THE NORMAN SOUTH DOORWAY, BARFRESTON CHURCH, KENT

51   THE NAVE OF ROCHESTER CATHEDRAL LOOKING EAST

52   BARGES   IN THE CREEK, LOWER HALSTOW, KENT

But it is time to get back to Watling Street, or, perhaps better, to the winding narrow road that follows the banks of the Medway by way of Lower Halstow, a place of brick-filled barges moored in a small creek (52). It is an artists' country just here, for you see the red sails of barges rising out of beds of green reeds and misty islands of grey.

As we come into Gillingham we see the deserted shell of "Jezreel's Temple" planned in 1885 by "God's last messenger to man", the soldier James White (James Jershon Jezreel), and his wife Queen Esther, whose real name sounds like that of a film star—Clarissa Rogers. White's attempt to gather together the last 144,000 descendants of the Israelites to escape death and live a further thousand years before going to heaven attracted some believers but not enough. The temple reached the third storey when funds failed.

Gillingham was a member of the Cinque Port of Hastings but has grown tremendously of late years.

Chatham, which stands to Gillingham much as Brighton stands to Hove, is of course famous for its three mile frontage of Dock-yards begun in the reign of Henry VIII and extended at different periods, the latest and largest being just seventy years ago.

Defoe described it as the most considerable arsenal in the world and the safest and best harbour in the world. There still remain many old houses in the narrow steep streets of the old town, that provide a strong contrast to the modern barracks of the Engineers and the old barracks of the Royal Marines.

The town is continuous with Rochester, which is a cathedral city of very great historic interest.

Here we have memories of the "Commodore" coach trans-porting Pickwick, Tupman, Winkle and Snodgrass from the *Silver Cross* in London to the *Bull Inn* at Rochester, which still preserves a Pickwickian atmosphere. The place is squalid enough, much of it, but it has an attraction individual, compelling, to think the wide river with its moored tiers of red sailed barges, the tremendous masonry of the Norman keep, and, by the cathedral, a surprising oasis of Georgian peace. The cathedral walls, like those of the magnificent Norman Keep, are blackened by dock-yard smoke, but inside the fabric is magnificent. The foundations of the original Saxon cathedral were laid by Ethelbert, the larger Norman cathedral begun by Gundulph. After Becket's murder the abbey became a roadside hostel for rich pilgrims. At the beginning of the thirteenth century a Scots baker after passing the night there was murdered and canonised as St. William of Perth, which led pilgrims to stop at his shrine and leave offerings, from the proceeds of which the present cathedral was enlarged and remodelled. Here is the silver shrine of Paulinus who has lain here for 800 years. You remember the story of the sparrow flitting into and out of the room and the old man who compared its passing

K

with the life of man. That was supposed to have taken place in the presence of Paulinus while he was trying to convert Edwin to Christianity, though it is also recounted of the Venerable Bede.

Rochester Cathedral boasts one of the best proportioned naves on a modest scale in England (51). It is pure Norman and rises on tier above tier of arches to a magnificent roof. The west doorway is very elaborate rich Norman work and is grandly carved. One of Rochester's rarest treasures is the 800 year old register of the Cathedral, the Textus Roffensis.

The mighty Keep of the Castle, also the work of Gundulph, stands 120 ft. high and 70 ft. square, and has the advantage of rising straight up from the river. Look out also for Eastgate House; where you may see the marks of a Roman chariot—the old Guildhall and the tall brick Restoration House, where Charles II slept the night before the Restoration, now a Town museum. There is a pleasant Stuart air about the street in which we find the Old Corn Exchange (1706), its projecting gilt clock, the gift of Sir Cloudesley Shovel, often Mayor. His portrait is in the Guildhall (1687) opposite the *Bull*. Here the exquisitely modelled gilt ship vane was placed on the cupola to commemorate him after his death in 1705; it came out far more costly than was anticipated, and there was a rare to-do as to how it was to be paid for (49). It is an exact model of his frigate *Rodney*, and is barque-rigged, measuring 6 ft. in length and as much in height.

North-west of Rochester between the Medway and the Thames there still remains a curiously undisturbed land, given wholly up to cultivation, a hedgeless expanse of thousands of acres of wheat, potatoes and grass, with not a shack to shock the eye.

There is little to tempt us to continue along Watling Street after Gad's Hill, so I turned aside there south-west to regain the hills. The spot where Sir John Falstaff robbed the Sandwich carriers and lied about it so blatantly to Prince Hal is marked by the picturesque inn bearing his name. On the opposite side of the road is the famous red brick house of Gad's Hill Place, where Dickens spent the last thirteen years of his life, now converted into a girls' school.

A footpath leads us into the deer park of Cobham with its magnificent chestnuts and ash trees, where stands an immense H-shaped red-brick mansion with tall twisted Tudor chimneys, Dutch gables, octagonal towers topped by cupolas and huge windows, built in the sixteenth century by Sir William Brooke, Lord Cobham, now the seat of Lord Darnley. It has a picture gallery 130 ft. long and a magnificent carved marble mantelpiece. In the village stands the picturesque and historic *Leather-Bottle* Inn, where Mr. Tracey Tupman entertained Winkle, Snodgrass and Pickwick after his disappointment over Rachel Wardle's elopement with Alfred Jingle.

The church, which has a fine Perpendicular battlemented tower is remarkable for the astonishing collection of Cobham brasses, which date from 1320 to 1529, and include that of Lady Joan Cobham, the oldest example but one of a brass of a lady in the country. There is a brass of a later Lady Joan, who had five husbands, one of whom was Sir John Oldcastle. There is an early thirteenth century chancel with encaustic tiles.

Behind the church we go through an archway and find ourselves on a little lawn surrounded by little white houses. This is Cobham College, a hospital for the poor. It stands on the crest of a hill overlooking undulating wooded country of great beauty that invites us to take the thin arrow-like ribbon footpath that stretches as far as the eye can see. It leads to the hamlet of Luddesdown, and Dowdes Church, which has had no congregation since the Black Death wiped out the population. Then I plunged through White House Wood to come out suddenly on to the Pilgrims' Way, here disfigured with shacks, with, however, a fine stone circle with two great monoliths forming a dolmen without a capstone. Thence I turned westward to Trottescliffe, where there is a church by a duck-pond near the site of an old palace, and again joined the great highway at Wrotham, the birthplace of Admiral Byng.

Wrotham, where the Archbishop of Canterbury used to have a Palace, possesses a church of very unusual interest.

It has a strongly buttressed Perpendicular tower with battlements, and a turret above the battlements, and underneath a vaulted passage to prevent the procession having to pass over unconsecrated ground. The nave is of exceptional breadth. There is a fifteenth century local-type screen, an Early English octagonal font and many brasses. The church bells in peace time play hymn tunes every three hours.

It is a mercy that Wrotham is by-passed by the coast road which now drops with well-engineered gradient from the North Downs, leaving it to the south.

Wrotham Heath, approached through deep sand banks covered with pines, picturesque peculiarity of this neighbourhood, has been ruined by bungalows.

South of the village of Ightham (53), where there are horse-box pews and good brasses in the fourteenth century church, and fine black and white houses in the square, lies one of the most lovely houses in England, Ightham Mote (2) (p. 68). It is extremely difficult to find, for there are winding deep hidden lanes and a maze of footpaths in these wooded sandy hills, leading downwards to nowhere and everywhere. Right at the bottom where the Bourne begins its journey to join the Medway stands this little stone and timber towered manor house of Ightham Mote, surrounded by a wide stretch of water and reached by two stone bridges, which lead under the great fifteenth century gateway of two storeys with a stone front and brick sides, to a small quadrangle with walls

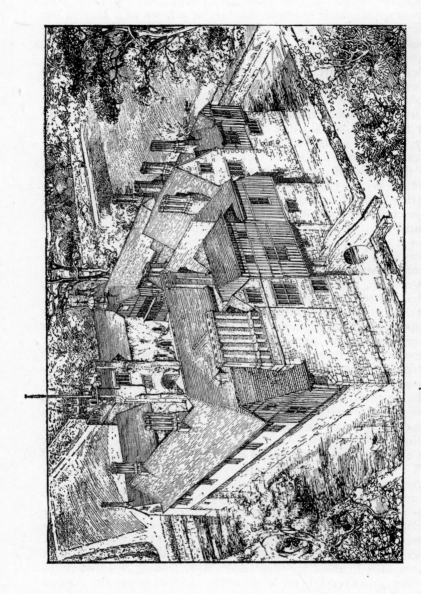

A BIRD'S-EYE VIEW OF IGHTHAM MOTE, KENT

covered with lichen and moss. There is a crypt which dates back
to the thirteenth century. The hall and kitchen stand as they have
stood since the fourteenth century, while the chapel was added in
the sixteenth century. There is a Jacobean drawing room and an
oriel-windowed banqueting hall that is quite perfect. Altogether
this secluded manor house breathes the very spirit of peace, yet it
was from here that a Lieutenant of the Tower rode out to meet
Richard III at Bosworth, and in the last war young Thomas
Colyer-Ferguson went out to gain a V.C. just before his death. It
bears points of resemblance to Queens' College, Cambridge, seen
from the Backs. Even in the summer of 1942 the house may be
seen from 3 to 6 on Fridays for 1s. a head, but at other times from
a public footpath which crosses in front and permits a close view
of the four fronts and the old stables.

Opposite the drive starts a cart track which passes by a large
sandstone farm with great fold yard, oast-houses and silos, and
continuously ascending through fruit fields leads to one of the
great views of Kent and of England. The difficulty is that, especially on the outer edge of the rising escarpment, thick belts of
woodland shut out all prospect, but between a field of badly laid
barley and an expanse of acres of a billowing yellowing wheat the
culmination is reached. Behind, rolling park-like country stretches
to a second sandy escarpment with the long line of the North
Downs beyond; in front is the vast dark green expanse of the
shallow Medway cleft—interrupted in one place by a large rising
patch of dense continuous woodland,—backed throughout by a
gentle rise to the heights of the Goudhurst country. There is a
surprising lack of building, except Hadlow's small patch of red
clustered at the foot of the squire's tower-folly, slender and high
enough to rank as the chimney of a public baths or refuse destruc-
tor, and where the raw extensions of Tonbridge town straggle up
the further slopes. The profusion of the abundant hedge timbering
masks the lighter green of the fields except directly to the south
where the horizon is bounded by an undulating clump-fringed
ridge. To the east the expanse grows flatter, more limitless and
paler as the eye ranges down the way that leads to the sea which
parts us from the enemy occupied coast. There must be some place
where the western view, completing an enormous half circle, can be
enjoyed, but my further experiences were unfortunate, and some time
would be needed for the discovery of a suitably clear accessible point.

A further point of interest in Ightham lies in the work of
Benjamin Harrison the grocer who devoted the whole of his life
to wandering on Oldbury Hill collecting thousands and thousands
of worked flints. He spent all his spare time on the hills and all his
working hours at his counter; and he was the discoverer in 1865
of the fact that our stone age ancestors went back much earlier
than the experts would then admit, and were great craftsmen in
flint-knapping.

We come out into the green land again at Shipbourne, a place of rhododendrons, the home of Sir Harry Vane of Fairlawn, now the seat of the Cazalets and the birthplace of that fine poet Christopher Smart, who wrote *The Song to David* with a piece of charcoal on the walls of the cell of the asylum in which he was shut up. His madness, as Dr. Johnson said, was not noxious. He merely prayed in the open streets and waylaid others to pray with him. Sir Harry Vane, after being Governor of Massachusetts at 24, was one of the few Roundheads whom Charles II sent to the scaffold by a shameful travesty of justice. "It is a bad cause that cannot bear the words of a dying man", was his last comment on his infamous verdict.

On the way into Tonbridge we may well turn aside to thread our way among the hop-fields and oast-houses to get a nearer view of the astonishing tall and slender modern "folly" tower of Hadlow Castle; in the church is the bishop's throne once occupied by Miles Coverdale, who collaborated with Tyndale to produce the English Bible. We are now in the valley of the Medway with the ancient town of Tonbridge lying in the bottom ahead.

Drawn by R. and J. A. Brandon

MERSTHAM CHURCH, SURREY, FROM THE SOUTH-EAST (*v. p.* 30)

TUNBRIDGE CASTLE.

From a Watercolour by Joseph Farington, R.A.

52a   THE CASTLE AND BRIDGE, TONBRIDGE, 1795

XI

TONBRIDGE TO WEST KENT

TUNBRIDGE WELLS has the advantage of being on the hill-tops, Tonbridge the advantage in history. I have no great love for the Medway, for its waters are sluggish and dirty, and the fascination of the hop-fields fades once the hops are picked. But Tonbridge itself possesses in its High Street, the red brick Tudor core of its largely Victorian Gothick Public School, and its Castle, three points of picturesque and historic interest. There are still some houses of interest in its busy High Street, such as the smartened half-timber Tudor *Chequers* Inn, and the demure Georgian *Rose and Crown*, largely the centre of local life.

It is the nursery of Kent cricketers, great sportsmen and happy warriors, and only spoilt by the traffic of those in a hurry to reach the sea.

North of it we are called by the wooded hills to Sevenoaks, whose street of irregular old houses sweeps up the steep slope of the Forest Ridge. The place is overshadowed by the vast park in which stands the great house of Knole (54–56). Sevenoaks has a cricket pitch that is 200 years old, and in its church are memories of three archbishops who lived at Knole. Building was started during the Wars of the Roses.

But the great glory of Sevenoaks lies in the vast house of Knole, the seat of the Sackvilles, first built by Archbishop Bouchier in the fifteenth century, but largely brought into its present size and form by the first Earl of Dorset, 1605–7 (54). The great triple quadrangular mansion is regularly shown in peace time; it is impossible here to do justice to its splendid suites of typical rich Early Renaissance interiors, and its endless treasures of furniture, silver, needlework and other craftsmanship (55, 56). These are, as when Walpole visited it, to quote his words "Ancient magnificence: loads of portraits, ebony cabinets, embossed silver in vases, dishes, etc., embroidered beds, stiff chairs, and sweet-bags lying on velvet tables, richly worked in silk and gold." The park, which is always open, covers nearly a thousand acres, and contains as fine a collection of giant oaks and beeches as I know. In the hollow of one of these a foundling was discovered to whom the name of William Sevenoke was given. He grew up to be Lord Mayor of London and founded the famous Grammar School in 1432 as well as the picturesque almshouses.

South-eastward from Sevenoaks stands an enchanted high land with triple peaks, culminating points of the sandy Forest Ridge: Ide Hill, Crookham Hill and Toy's Hill, which, rising just to 800 ft. at one point, the highest in all Kent, provide the richest views in all this very rich garden of England. The view point at Ide Hill is laid out for a war memorial as a little park full of

yellow broom and silver birches, while at Toy's Hill we get the
earliest of the lands specially preserved for the nation by the
National Trust. From here it is possible to see over seven counties
on a clear day; with a view most vast and dramatic to the south,
across the wide Eden–Medway Valley to the wooded heathland
heights of Ashdown Forest.

On the side of the hill to the west stands, looking out on this
superb view, the large red brick house of Winston Churchill,
"Chartwell". Behind it to the north run lovely tracks through
dense woods and over commons and heaths, by means of which
we work our way northward, and between the chalk and the sand
eventually find ourselves looking over on the fair village-town of
Westerham, an admirable centre for lovers of quiet walks. It was
here that William Pitt lived and Wolfe of Quebec was born in the
white vicarage, to be brought up at Quebec House, which now
belongs to the National Trust.

The over-restored church is fourteenth century, a typical
Kentish type building with its three parallel naves, no clerestory,
short tower and broach spire. It stands up splendidly above the
main broad ancient street, and contains a great collection of
brasses. At one end of the village stands the green, and at the
other a delectable pond, and the river Darent rises in the park
that surrounds the Georgian house of Squerryes Court, which is
encircled by peculiarly tall Spanish chestnuts. The elaborate
original lay-out of garden and grounds has vanished, but lives for
us in Badeslade's view of *ca.* 1720.

North of these enchanting hills on the south of Westerham and
Brasted needs wary walking, for though there is plenty of open
country and natural beauty, there is also a great deal of suburban
development and disfigurement. The pleasant northward curving
narrow valley of the Darent, just risen in Squerryes Park, is an
exception, so let us first follow that for its course of twenty miles
to the Thames at Dartford.

The walk begins at Brasted with a fine wide street and the
stately Classic House of Brasted Place, built by Adam for a King's
doctor, and later the home of Louis Napoleon.

The Pilgrims' Way, now diverted, formerly ran along the north
bank of the river through Chevening Park close by the house,
once attributed like many another to Inigo Jones, but greatly
enlarged and altered, rich in manuscripts of Byron and Lord
Chesterfield. The house has now two subsidiary blocks with
curved connections to the main block, painfully cased in patent
tiles by the third Earl. There is a staircase by Nicholas Dubois,
and fine wood panel interiors, one with a set of tapestries presented
by Frederick the Great.

The Pilgrims' Way crosses the wide gap in the downs made by
the Darent at Otford, where the few remains of the Tudor Palace
stand up finely above the meadows. The Romans had a settlement

53   IGHTHAM VILLAGE, KENT

54 KNOLE HOUSE, SEVENOAKS

here, and it was here that Offa beat the men of Kent, and later Canute was defeated by Edmund Ironside at their fifth battle.

The Palace, which aroused the jealous eye of Henry VIII, was vastly enlarged at a cost of £33,000, a figure which now might be perhaps ten times as much, by Warham. It had been the Palace of Archbishops from Becket to Cranmer, who handed it over to Henry VIII, who decided that while he was at Knole his household could live in Otford. It was stripped of its lead roofing and fell into decay shortly after his death. The village also possesses a black and white manor house, and an old inn enriched by panelling from the Palace.

Otford Church has a square squat tower, built of flint and rag, plastered and patched with red brick, and surmounted by a blunt shingled spire. It has a seventeenth century gabled porch of timber, and a Jacobean octagonal font.

The view from the churchyard of the surrounding downlands is exceptionally wide and full of charm, a view that increases in beauty as we take the river bank walk northward along the Darent to the picturesque village of Shoreham. The church here is mainly Perpendicular with a nave floor that slopes considerably upwards towards the east. Its great treasure is its very rich wood screen that retains the original vaulting and extends across the chancel and south chapel with eight bays and vine ornamentation. It is generally considered to be the most perfect old screen in Kent.

The whole setting of Shoreham is attractive, and it is not to be wondered that artists should always have shown much affection for it. Everywhere there are groupings of thatched barns under tall elms, Tudor houses with high stacked chimneys, and always there is the winding water with gardens running down to the river bank, and the rising uplands of the chalk downs on both sides of the valley.

And it is possible to recover a purely mediaeval atmosphere at Eynsford, where stands the old narrow bridge with overhanging timbered cottages untouched by modernity, and one can look far afield over the richly wooded valley of the Darent without seeing a single eyesore of red brick settlements. Eynsford's Little Mote, on the river bank close by the castle, is pure Tudor within and without. Obviously Eynsford was once a most important ford.

The Norman castle has now only its extensive outer walls surviving. In a garden on Eynsford Hill many Roman items have been found. The church has a partly Norman tower, covered with a lofty shingled spire, a fifteenth century porch whose side pillars have twisted mouldings, and above, an earlier round arch of four moulded orders. In the Early English south transept are eight deep-splayed lancets, and there is also an octagonal Perpendicular font.

The way on to Farningham takes us through Sparepenny Lane,

L

still completely unspoilt. Farningham, cut up and with much modern building, has in spite of its arterial road preserved its old mill, manor house and flint-towered church, where rest Colyers and Ropers, close to an octagonal fifteenth century font which has figure carvings on all its sides; they represent the seven sacraments, a form common in East Anglia, but very rare in southeast England.

Farningham Church has an Early English chancel, a fifteenth century flint and stone tower, octagonal font and three good brasses.

Opposite *The Lion* there is a board-fronted flour mill, now converted into a private house, that spans the mill stream, and in the garden of *The Lion* there is a high pitched three-arched screen of red brick put up to protect the ford. This screen had hurdles across the arches to prevent loss of cattle and sheep in flood time. The general compactness and snugness of this warm red brick village can best be appreciated from the wide arterial by-pass that makes a half-circle round its eastern boundary. It is today perhaps the nearest of Kent's beauty spots to London.

Here too, with lawns running down to the river which sweeps round a tiny island, is the great Tudor house of Franks, built by Alderman Bathurst in Eliabethan days; it was long a farmhouse, and in spite of some Victorianising in its restoration to a country house, it has many fine features. A large monograph with specially taken photographs was devoted to it some years ago.

Just here lies Dartford with its tower of Gundulf, workshop of Trevethick, and Wat Tyler's cottage. It also possesses a curious little harbour that comes as an entire surprise. It was almost the first town to provide us with paper; today, it also produces powder, chemicals and general machinery. Anne of Cleves spent the last seven years of her life in the priory, and Martin Frobisher came to see the mills and furnaces of his time that surrounded it.

In the great church, which has an eleventh century tower, is the tomb of Sir John Spielman, Queen Elizabeth's Jeweller, who founded the first paper mill in Kent, one of the earliest in England, and a host of splendid brasses. And high above the Norman tower on the hill where Chaucer's pilgrims rested in a vanished chantry stands the tower of the Martyrs' Memorial.

Dartford has spread enormously, largely in streets of small suburban houses, and there are vast factories of not unattractive modern design. It is fitting that paper and engineering should be prominent industries here and along the Thames Estuary, for Dartford was connected with great pioneer figures in both. First, Sir John Spielman who is a century ahead of the Evelyns at Chilworth; then, Richard Trevethick, that tragic and brilliant engineering genius who was the first to run a really practicable locomotive, as well as to produce other outstanding achievements. After a century of almost complete forgetfulness a generously

55   THE JAMES I ROOM   56   LADY SACKVILLE'S ROOM, WITH THE SILVER TOILET SET

57   CHURCH COBHAM, SURREY: THE RIVER MOLE AND THE CHURCH

58   A KENTISH CHERRY ORCHARD

worded tablet to him, instigated by well wishers across the Atlantic, was placed in the parish church where he was buried. The curious forms of early steamship engines were originally made here and at Greenwich; with the transfer of ship building to the North, it is the wide field of accessory engines which is worked on the Thames.

Thus Dartford's busy present has almost extinguished the signs of its honourable past, and we shall do well here to turn southwest towards what is left of the once rustic glories of the Crays and Keston Pond, to regain the high chalk land at Downe, where we can still see in the square white house the study in which Darwin wrote, left exactly as in his life-time, and walk among the quiet pleasant gardens where he worked in a quietude that makes it difficult to believe that we are only sixteen miles from London Bridge.

In the old church you will find the tombs of Sir John and Lady Lubbock, parents of that Lord Avebury, ("St. Lubbock" of Bank Holiday fame) who was Darwin's dearest friend. And so by way of Cudham with its tall spire that looks down on the whole Weald of Kent, and two most ancient yews, we come over Westerham Hill to cross the border as we move into Surrey at the very point that we left it.

Drawn by R. and J. A. Brandon

NORTH MIMMS CHURCH, HERTFORDSHIRE (*v. page* 115)

XII

WESTERHAM TO WINDSOR

THIS is a journey that needs wary walking, for though there are golden things to see on the way, one false turn may transport you from an untouched common to a suburban high street, from the quietude of a still unspoilt village to the unpleasant liveliness of an arterial road. It is a good walking rule to keep on the chalk heights as long as possible between Westerham and Reigate, and then make a line for Walton-on-the-Hill or Great Bookham, where there are still geese on the common and we are free to walk through the woodland rides beneath the shade of giant oaks and silver birches.

Just north of the slopes of the North Downs is Great Bookham, which has an unspoilt rural church with shingled broach spire, its chancel built by John de Rutherwyke, Abbot of Chertsey in 1341, with a Latin inscription deeply cut in beautiful Lombardie lettering in the interior to the east. The twelfth century font is of Petworth marble, and there are brasses of the Slyfields and a grotesque monument to Colonel Thomas Moore dated 1735, in which his uniform appears to be a mixture of bathing costume, kilt and plaid. In the Slyfield Chapel there are more monuments to the Slyfield family as well as to the Howards of Effingham.

The former manor house of Slyfield on the banks of the Mole is now a farmhouse, but it is still a fine example of mid-seventeenth century brickwork and has boldly modelled plaster ceilings and a carved staircase. There is a good deal of this interesting mid-Stuart brickwork in Surrey, executed with sterling craftsmanship. We need only refer to the work in Godalming High Street and the house of 1636 at Mickleham.

Just north is Stoke d'Abernon, a well-wooded village on the north bank of the Mole, with a church that is still full of interest in spite of a horrible restoration in 1866. Luckily some of the south Saxon wall is preserved, as well as the Saxon square-headed blocked-up doorway which formed, high up, the entrance to a priest's chamber, and the Saxon sun dial. There is a fine mural painting, and the Norbury chantry was put up in the reign of Henry VII. There is an original fireplace in the north wall that is a very unusual feature of a Pre-Reformation chapel, but it is the monuments that chiefly draw the sightseer. Here is the earliest known English brass, to Sir John D'Abernon, dated 1277, and another to his son of the same name dated 1327. Two other small brasses are fixed to the stone panelled ends of the niche of Sir John Norbury's vanished tomb, of which the quaint brass inscription remains. There is also a Cross of Thomas Lyfelde 1592 with a long genealogical inscription, another to John Pynnoke, the first

priest of the chantry, dated 1521. There are clumsy effigies under
great canopies of Sarah Lady Vincent, 1608, and to Sir Thomas
and Lady Vincent, 1623. Among other treasures is the finest
thirteenth century chest known, and an elaborately carved seven-
sided Jacobean pulpit with a sounding-board with rich iron stays,
and an hourglass stand on the wall.

There are lovely walks along the water-meadows to Church
Cobham (57) and Street Cobham, a place of red-roofed warm brick
and timbered houses, some overlooking a common, and some
with pleasant tree-fringed gardens. Especially attractive are the old
Church-stile Houses that stands by the lych-gate of the church,
built in 1432 and restored in 1635, and the old posting house, *The
White Lion*, that has stood for over 400 years.

There is a pleasant walk from here over commons and through
woods that leads over the Wey to Pyrford, where the little restored
church overlooks the ruins of Newark Priory, whose roofless walls
stands above the water where it divides into seven streams (17).
It was built at the end of the twelfth century, surrendered in
1538, and now is just a shell of south transept walls and three
choir bays.

Nearby is Send, including a church with a fifteenth century
tower and nave, and brasses to the Slyfield family dated 1521.

Ripley's broad street is spoilt by being on the Portsmouth Road,
but when it is quiet, in the evening and early morning, one gets a
chance to appreciate its large green and fine red brick and timbered inns and other houses (60). *The Anchor Inn*, a once famous
cycling resort, is a good old gabled house, though more restless
as restored with its timbering exposed than in its former plaster
coat, and Hole's Cottage, once the manor house, has good seventeenth century brickwork.

Modern Woking has little to recommend it; at Old Woking the
church has a fine Norman doorway, and nearby is the great
house of Sutton Place, erected by Sir Richard Weston between
1523 and 1525. It is built entirely of brick with fine detail in
lighter terracotta Gothick with Renaissance touches, and originally
formed a quadrangle. The long gallery was restored in 1875 by
Frederick Harrison, who published an illustrated monograph on
the house called *Annals of an old Manor house*; later it was
acquired by the Harmsworth family.

The most attractive country near Woking lies on the north
side, where we come to a really wild stretch of commons
with deserted thickets and lovely tall pines at Chobham Ridges.
The church has been drastically restored, but the tower dates
from the early fifteenth century. An Archbishop of York,
Nicholas Heath, described by Fuller as "a meek and modest
man carrying a Court of Conscience in his bosom" lies
buried here. Chobham Place is famous for its firs and Spanish
chestnuts.

There are miles of open walks and rides over the Ridges, leading either westward to even wilder Bagshot Heath, or to the smiling rhododendron-fringed common of Ascot Heath.

Northward at Egham we come to a dingy amorphous church and a long street of houses that have been none too happily treated, but just outside is the moat-encircled late Tudor house of Great Fosters, built as a hunting lodge for Queen Elizabeth. In dramatic contrast is the enormous and extraordinary building up the hill. Of red brick with stone dressings, it is Holloway College, and is a late Victorian version of Francis I's Château de Chambord. Its cost was defrayed out of a fortune made out of pills, and it now functions usefully as a training centre for girl teachers.

We are now on the fringes of Virginia Water, where a most delightful public walk under tall trees encircles the Great Lake, the largest artificial sheet of water in the Kingdom, made in 1746 by damming up and diverting a number of small streams. There is the Hermitage, the triangular turreted Belvedere, with guns used by Cumberland in the '45, and a Swiss chalet replacing the Chinese fishing temple from which George III used daily to angle, while a miniature frigate sailed on the lake. But in contrast to these garden adornments is the colonnade of granite, marble and porphyry brought from the ruins of Leptis Major near Tripoli (66). It is said that an Italian archaelogist acquaintance of the late King George V petitioned for their restoration to their original site, but apparently the negotiations were not completed. Here we get an example of artificial landscape gardening on a most lavish scale, and lovers of the natural will probably be glad to escape to the untouched thousands of acres that lead on past royal farms and fields to the Great Park of Windsor, where we pass out of Surrey into Berkshire.

Drawn by Roland W. Paul, F.R.I.B.A

GREENSTEAD-JUXTA-ONGAR CHURCH, ESSEX (*v. page* 117)

59 BARGES ON THE WEY, NEAR WEYBRIDGE, SURREY

60 THE COURTYARD OF THE TALBOT INN, RIPLEY, SURREY

61 THE CHURCH AND CITY STONE, STAINES, 120 YEARS AGO

By Richard Havell

62 DATCHET FERRY, NEAR WINDSOR, 120 YEARS AGO

By Richard Havell

XIII

THE THAMES FROM MAIDENHEAD
TO KEW

IT is only natural that the great mother river should be as compact
of history as of beauty. It is not only in the halcyon days of summer
when we lie idly in a punt or canoe under tall poplars and the
overhanging willows, letting the world and the water go slipping
smoothly and dreamily by, but in the more strenuous walking
days of winter that the Thames banks reveal their mystery and
charm.

An excellent starting place is Maidenhead below the woods on
the cliffs of Cliveden. Nearby is Bray, a pleasant village of old
houses and a cottage over the lych gate to the churchyard, famous
for its vicar, the turncoat Simon Aleyn, whose chameleon nature
gave rise to one of our more famous ballads. He managed to live
safely through the reigns of Henry VIII, Edward VI, Mary and
Eliabeth, no mean achievement. In his church are eight brasses,
one of the founder of the Tudor brick almshouses (The Jesus
Hospital) whose quadrangle is well known as the scene of a famous
picture by Frederick Walker.

At Boveney we do well to leave the river to explore the magnificent Beeches of Burnham, which lead us to the rose-covered
churchyard at Stoke Poges, the scene of Thomas Gray's famous
elegy, Gray himself is commemorated by a grotesque sarcophagus,
as ugly as his poem is beautiful, erected by John Penn. But there
is compensation in Gray's own simple tomb, where he lies by the
side of the mother whom he so dearly loved.

Close by the church, recently deprived of its spire, is the old
manor house, once the home of Sir Christopher Hatton, and later
of the famous Coke who sent Raleigh to his death. Charles I was
imprisoned in it, and in 1760 it was bought by the son of William
Penn, who signed the treaty with the Indians under the trunk of
an elm that still stands. A modern cloister full of heraldic glass is
connected with the beautifully kept church, which must be the
most frequently visited of all village churches in England. Stoke
Court, a fine Adam period place, is now a country club.

Towering over the landscape by the river, to which we now
return, is the Royal Castle of Windsor with its countless memories
from Herne the Hunter to our own day (10). It was William of
Wykeham who gave the castle most of its Tudor shape, but it has
been continually added to since his day, and it was largely transformed in the early nineteenth century by Sir Geoffrey Wyattville,
nephew of the James Wyatt whom we shall meet in Hertfordshire

at Ashridge. It has been the home of all our Kings since Henry I.
It was here that the Black Prince and Henry VI were born, that
James I of Scotland saw from his cell the lovely Jane Beaufort
with whom he fell in love and later married. In St. George's
Chapel, whose tall pillars rise so delicately to one of the finest and
most individual vaults in the Kingdom, are buried Henry VIII,
Charles I and Edward VII.

Here is the dark chapel of the Knights of the Garter lit up by
the multi-coloured banners and swords of the possessors of this
most cherished order; above stands the Curfew Tower with its
reminders of the cruelties to which its helpless captives were
subjected. Sixteen of the main rooms in the Royal apartments are
open to the public.

Here we are apt to become so confused by the wealth of old
masters that it is a relief to ascend the Round Tower and look out
on all the magnificence of Windsor Great Park, the winding
poplar-fringed Thames, the red brick clustering buildings of Eton,
and, further afield, on an outstanding view which ranges over
twelve counties. From here we look down a double avenue of
elms that stretches for a straight three miles to the great equestrian
statue of George III.

On the further side of the park lies Old Windsor, where Edward
the Confessor built a palace, with a famous inn *The Bells of Ouseley*,
a churchyard in which lies the lovely actress and King's mistress,
Mary Robinson, better known as Perdita, whose beauty lives for
ever in the portraits of Romney, Reynolds and Gainsborough.

But the most cherished memory of Windsor is not roaming
among the deer in a park that covers 13,000 acres, but in those
golden moments spent on the wide terraces listening to the band
of the Brigade of Guards.

Down by the river below the great walls of the Castle stands
Eton with its magnificent chapel built in 1476 (63),—which
inevitably invites comparison with the peerless chapel of King's
Cambridge,—two mellowed brick quadrangles and cloisters built
in 1523, all with memories of a long line of statesmen, poets and
warriors which no other Public School can hope to rival. In the
Lower School you may see their initials carved in the desks and
the famous flogging-block where they received one part of their
education. The Upper School was Wren's work, and in it are
busts of Pitt, Fox, Fielding, Gladstone, Shelley and other eminent
Etonians.

In the second quadrangle is the College Dining Hall and the
Fellows' Library, a long L-shaped room of great dignity in which
are housed many rarities, including a First Folio Shakespeare. In
the School library, a rotunda reminiscent of the Radcliffe Camera
at Oxford, is the original manuscript of Gray's *Elegy*. Within a
stone's throw, beautifully situated among tall trees on the river
bank, are the famous playing fields.

Drawn by Roland W. Paul, F.R.I.B.A.

ETON COLLEGE CHAPEL, THE NORTH SIDE

There are many islets in the river near here where the "swan-upping" excursions to mark the cygnets provide an annual ceremony of unusual interest. It was at Datchet Mead that Falstaff was thrown into the ditch by the Merry Wives, and on the south bank lies the wide field of Runnymede where King John signed Magna Carta, the foundation of all our liberties.

Just to the south of Egham, best reached by walking across the Great Park, stands the great lake of Virginia Water, a beautiful tree-fringed water, which we have already visited (p. 78). Opposite Runnymede stands Magna Carta Island and the yew of Ankerwyke where Henry VIII used to meet Anne Boleyn.

Just after Bell Weir Lock we come to Staines, an unsightly medley of gasworks and reservoirs from which it is pleasant to turn aside up the Colnbrook to the spoilt village of that name where Elizabeth slept one night as a prisoner at *The George Inn*, and Catherine in the *Catherine Wheel*. *The Ostrich* is, or was, another fine inn of timber with memories of highwaymen.

Just ahead lies Horton where John Milton wrote *L'Allegro*, *Il Penseroso*, *Comus*, and *Lycidas*, and was certainly inspired to write these excellently descriptive lines that so well conjure up this reach of the river:—

> "Meadows trim with daisies pied;
> Shallow brooks and rivers wide,
> Towers and battlements it sees
> Bosomed high in tufted trees,
> Where perhaps some beauty lies,
> The cynosure of neighbouring eyes."

The poet's mother was buried here in the churchyard, which has an exceptionally fine old yew. On the Middlesex bank of the Thames the next place of interest is Laleham, the birthplace of another poet, Matthew Arnold, whose deep appreciative feeling for the Thames is, as is well known, one of his chief characteristics.

And so we come to Chertsey with the poor scanty remains of an Abbey that was founded in 666, and is famed for the special splendour of its thirteenth century encaustic tiles, a riverside town of old red roofs and picturesque houses that has somehow managed to keep some of its mediaeval spirit. Curfew is still rung through the winter. Above stands St. Anne's Hill, once the home of C. J. Fox, and in Guildford Street you may see still Abraham Cowley's home in the Jacobean Porch House; the porch went in 1786, and the house is now named after the poet. It is still possible to find a quiet and pleasant walk to Shepperton, a typical angler's haunt with old inns, handsome houses, and a churchyard in which lies the body of the three-year-old daughter of Thomas Love Peacock.

Weybridge is certainly not what it was thirty years ago, for Brooklands racing track among such other things as multitudes of good new villa houses has altered it, but there are still un-

63 ETON COLLEGE AND CHAPEL, *ca.* 1820

touched pinewoods and open heaths, and the side of Oatlands
Park, once a palace of Henry VIII, now occupied by an hotel. The
appearance of the Old Palace can best be visualised by Wyngaarde's
drawings in the Bodleian Library, Oxford.

The church at Walton where once was the home of Sir Arthur
Sullivan is worth visiting for the sake of fourteenth century chancel,
fifteenth century tower and monuments, but Halliford with its
green and old houses, one of them the home of Peacock, has a
much greater attraction.

The next village on the Middlesex side is Sunbury, a warm-
looking place of prosperous pleasant houses of red brick with red
tiled roofs, where Oliver Twist and Bill Sikes slept the night
before the burglary.

Two race-courses here face each other on opposite sides of the
river, Kempton Park on the Middlesex bank and Hurst Park close
by the junction of the enchanting Mole and the Thames.

Then comes Hampton, with the house that the Adam Brothers
enlarged for David Garrick, with its famous octagonal domed
summer-house known as the Shakespeare Temple. In byegone
days Hampton was a favourite place of the great men, for Sir
Richard Steele lived in "The Hovel", and other houses were the
homes of Sir Christopher Wren, Nell Gwyn's son and the first
Lord Lytton. And little wonder, for here stands the lovely park of
Bushy, which calls all London to come and admire its lime and
chestnut avenue, running for a straight mile to link up Teddington
with the Lion Gates of Hampton Court Palace. In Hampton
Church are monuments to Mrs. Jordan and her son by William IV,
Lord Fitzclarence, Garrick and Edward VI's nurse, who still
haunts Hampton Court. Close by is Hanworth, the home of
Katherine Parr after her marriage to Sir Thomas Seymour.

But the great feature of this neighbourhood is of course Hampton Court, one of the most superb of Wolsey Palaces. It was here
that Henry VIII brought Anne Boleyn, that Edward VI was born
and that other of Henry's wives endured the attention and neglect
of their capricious Lord.

Elizabeth, who had good reason to hate Hampton, was brought
here as a prisoner from Woodstock, and later when she came to
the throne decided here the fate of Mary, Queen of Scots. James I
spent his first English Christmas here, and Charles I who used it
as an escape from the Plague, was also held here as prisoner.
Cromwell found it a pleasant home, and Charles II also liked it
enough to cut the long canal, and plant it with limes and yews; it
was here he entertained Pepys and Lely.

Most of the changes we now see were wrought by Sir Christopher
Wren at the command of William of Orange, and the magnificently laid out grounds are mainly his work. George I kept it as
a place of dalliance with his mistresses, but George III refused to
live in it, and in Victoria's reign it was thrown open to the public.

I know few places which give one so vividly the sense of being largely populated by royal ghosts, and few places where on each visit I am so struck afresh by its magnificence.

The deep red brick of its walls, its Tudor chimneys, its succession of quadrangles, its imposing battlemented gateway with the splendid oriel window over the porch, its surroundings of bowers, sunken gardens, great vine and even the maze (which is what attracts nine-tenths of the crowd) all contrive to make it a feast to the eye that never wearies. The key, by the way, to the maze is to take every turning to the left after taking the first two turns to the right (p. 86).

It is impossible to do more than refer to its superb craftsmanship in the two noblest of English indigenous styles, Tudor and late Stuart. The ironwork is by the Huguenot refugee, Jean Tijou, and there is a vast range of wood panelled interiors, with ceilings often painted by Verrio and Laguerre. One curious touch is shown by some of the fire-backs, whose markings of IR 1687 show that the thrifty Dutch William used his dispossessed father-in-law's gear.

The river and the houseboats from here on are much less popular since the coming of the motor car to take holiday-makers further afield, and indeed there is not much recompense to make up for the amazing spread of stereotyped suburbanisation which has eaten so much of that ancient fair land on Thames side.

You would hardly guess that no fewer than seven Saxon kings were crowned at bustling modern Kingston, yet their Coronation Stone is still to be seen, painfully within railings, on a seven-sided base of granite. It was here that Sir Thomas Wyatt led his rebels across the Thames in his attack on London. The church, which was destroyed by lightning in 1445, still contains fifteenth century brasses and interesting monuments. The Grammar School of Queen Elizabeth occupies the Chapel of St. Mary Magdalen built in 1304. Kingston Market is attractive, and I have known Londoners in peace time drive out here for flowers, vegetables and old furniture and antiques.

At Teddington we have reminders of R. D. Blackmore, who had a market-garden, Thomas Treherne who lies buried here and Richard Bentley whose friend Horace Walpole lived at Strawberry Hill. "It is set," he said, "in enamelled meadows with filigree hedges." He lived in this favourite sham Gothick mansion for fifty years and wrote his *Castle of Otranto* here. It was here that he gathered around him all the notables of the century, and after his death bequeathed the property to the sisters Agnes and Mary Berry, his most intimate friends.

Indeed this area of Twickenham, now given up to Rugby football, exercised a strange fascination over eighteenth century Londoners. Dickens wrote *Oliver Twist* at Ailsa Villa, Fielding wrote *Tom Jones* in Holly Road; Swift, Tennyson, J. M. W. Turner and Chantry all lived here.

Indeed there was truth in the couplet:

> "Twick'nam the Muses' fav'rite seat
> Twick'nam the Graces' loved retreat."

The church in which Pope, Admiral Byron, and Kitty Clive all lie buried is the successor of one built by William of Wykeham that fell down in 1713. Its most famous house was of course Pope's, with its extraordinary grotto that he decorated with shells. It was pulled down about 110 years ago by Lady Howe, who was annoyed by visits from the poet's many admirers. Henry Labouchere lived here in the house that now occupies the spot. Orleans House with its charming gardens was once the home of Louis Philippe. Marble Hill was built by George II for Mrs. Howard, and afterwards became the home of Mrs. Fitzherbert and Sir Robert Peel before being acquired by the L.C.C. It has a noble series of Palladian interiors, and the staircase is impressively fine; they should be visited. Queen Anne was born in York House. Of the attractions of Eel Pie Island and similar popular resorts that stud these reaches, I am not qualified to speak, for they are not to me attractive. On the other hand, I have a great affection for Richmond (64), partly by reason of its great wooded deer park and partly because in spite of its activity and modernity, it has somehow contrived to preserve in its gardens and terraces some trace of the old world and some of its old architectural loveliness.

In the royal palace of Sheen, Henry VII and Elizabeth both died. Only the gateway remains, and a small piece of building incorporating some mixed interiors. As at Oatlands, the old palace lives for us again in Wyngaarde's fine drawings at the Bodleian Library. There are also a painting at the Fitzwilliam Museum, Cambridge, and many lesser engravings. James Thomson, author of *The Seasons*, was buried in the Parish Church. Maid of Honour Row is a pleasant Restoration Terrace fronting a wide green; there are some agreeable Georgian houses.

The view of the curve of the tree-fringed Thames from Richmond Hill still remains as it was when it drew that fine panegyric from Sir Walter Scott in *The Heart of Midlothian* and continues deservedly to attract countless artists. And at the far end of the Old Deer Park we are at the gates of Kew, which is lovely not only in lilac-time. Kew Palace was the home of George III's mother, and it was at his command that these magnificent botanical gardens were laid out in 1760. In the churchyard you will find the grave of Gainsborough who died here in 1788.

We are now too near London to tempt the water any further, but before we leave we may look across at Hounslow and recall that it was not very long ago that this then lonely heath was the favourite haunt of plover and highwayman. Near by at Isleworth are the finely wooded grounds of quadrangular Syon House, where Lady Jane Grey was proclaimed Queen, and the red brick home of Lord Jersey, Osterley Park, also famous for its trees, though Horace Walpole described it as the ugliest spot of ground in the universe. Both these houses, though not remarkable in their exteriors, are outstanding for their splendid suites of rich interiors, which represent the highest type of Robert Adam's delicate classic design.

And at Brentford, which you would scarcely guess is the capital of Middlesex, long famous for its grubby appearance, we may well exchange the river for the canal, for here is the head-quarters of the working boatmen and bargemen, who ply their gaily painted, brightly burnished craft between here and the industrial Midlands at a tempo that we all envy and might with advantage imitate.

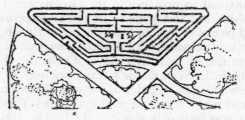

Drawn by H. Inigo Triggs

PLAN OF HAMPTON COURT MAZE (*v. page* 84)

64 RICHMOND BY THE BRIDGE, 1790

XIV

A CIRCULAR TOUR FROM GERRARD'S CROSS

A GOOD starting point from which to begin to ramble among some typical stretches of Buckinghamshire, the long sweeps of beech-covered Chiltern Hills with their wide peaceful valleys is I think Gerrard's Cross, for Gerrard's Cross is the first place on the London–Oxford Road which is really outside the metropolis.

Since it became accessible by the new joint line some years ago, many fairly well-designed houses and large gardens have appeared, but not far off such typical spots as Seer Green and Austenwood Common still keep a country air.

St. James' church is one of those curious Victorian white brick Italianate affairs with dome and campanile that can never look anything but exotic and incongruous. It has its fellows at Oxford, Wilton, Hoarwithy and Eastbourne.

Its common still stands with its bracken and gorse and haw-thorn undisturbed, and there are footpaths leading off across fields and parks to villages that are still villages and not mushroom growths of new flats and multiple stores. Such as Fulmer and Hedgerley, and not far off is Stoke Poges with its churchyard memories of Gray on which we have already touched; it is still possible to work one's way here from the Bath Road at Slough by quiet by-lanes through restful country stretches without passing even a hamlet or touching so much as a spot of suburbanised wretchedness.

The hills start their gentle rise above the river joinings at Uxbridge, and Denham, fortunately preserved on its loop off the main road, is a village of distinctive attraction, and the huge Denham film sheds stand well apart. Denham Place, long the seat of the Ways, is a fine red brick Restoration house with a lake in its grounds; the interior has much fine wood panelling and modelled plasterwork.

The film studios used to be in the habit of distributing their characters round about: you might meet Queen Elizabeth and her maids of honour on Gerrard's Cross Common, and see her sweep in starched ruff and paniered skirt into a high powered car and whirl away.

On the further side of the common is Bulstrode Park, of which a portion was recently given over for sites for quite pleasant houses; it was once the home of Judge Jeffreys, who built himself a house there in 1686. It passed into the hands of the Dukes of Portland and Somerset, and latterly to Sir John Ramsden; the present vast deserted house is a dreary essay in arid Victorian.

Ahead lies Beaconsfield, still one of the most attractive little towns in the Home Counties, with its wide, clean streets, red roofed, neat and rich looking houses and large over-restored church, famous as the burial place of Edmund Burke, who lived at Butler's Court, and Edmund Waller of Hall Barn, where the late Lord Burnham used to entertain Edward VII.

On the way to Beaconsfield the road skirts Wilton Park with its great splendid beech trees; a public footpath crosses it in the direction of Seer Green, in a district of many cherry orchards, and Jordans, with its beautifully preserved Quaker meeting house and burial ground; among the simple headstones are those of William Penn and his first wife Guilelma Springett. An ill-judged iconoclastic proposal to run an important road past its secluded peace was mercifully defeated recently.

Just beyond Beaconsfield a road leads north through a beech wood to Penn, an attractive upland village near the vast Penn Wood on a ridge from which you look over the Thames valley to Windsor. There is a farm at the entrance to the village with an arresting notice over the doorway asking the reader to respect the Sabbath. The church, which has a fine timber roof, contains hatchments of Queen Anne and the Curzons, and some very interesting brasses of the Penn family. Just beyond is Penn Street with a pond and an Independent Meeting House, and near below is the busy town of High Wycombe with its immensely long street, famous girls' school at Wycombe Abbey, and fine church built partly by the Abbess of Godstow in 1273, containing a costly tomb to Henry Pelly, Earl of Shelbourne. It is the largest church in the county (as this High or Chipping Wycombe is the largest town) a well proportioned mid-mediaeval fabric with a tower altered in Renaissance style. Wycombe has grown enormously in the last twenty years; spreading up the slopes of the hill-sides it is the greatest centre of furniture making in the country, in many forms and styles, with the plain Windsor chair perhaps predominating. The traditional method is still carried on by which the legs and stretchers are largely turned on the old pole-lathes in sheds of the hamlets on the hills and sent down to the town to be assembled. The old primitive system of bodgering or chair-turning in temporary sheds in the woods is still occasionally met with, but has largely died out. Recently a group of bodgers near Stoke Row were very active,—turning out hundreds of tent pegs! There are still some eighteenth century pieces in the by-streets, but Londonwards extends a continuous succession of regrettably unattractive hamlets which slow down through traffic for an unbroken five miles of built-up area. The circular Market House and Georgian Town Hall with centaur vane give some indication of the town's ancient standing, but are rather cramped by the congestion of other less worthy buildings and heavy traffic. Close by is Hughenden, the home and burial place of

65   MAGNOLIA AND DAFFODILS BY A TEMPLE, KEW GARDENS

66   THE RUINS, VIRGINIA WATER

67 WENDOVER UNDER BODDINGTON HILL ON THE CHILTERN ESCARPMENT, FROM COOMBE HILL

Disraeli. Here too lies his wife, and Sarah Brydges Willyams who
left him £40,000 because she liked his words so much. The monument to him was erected by "his grateful sovereign and friend,
Victoria R.I. *Kings Love him that Speaketh Right*". The interest of
the place lies more in its associations than in its intrinsic attractions, but the church has other noteworthy monuments, including
the tombs of an Abbot of Kenilworth, and an illegitimate son of
Simon de Montfort. Isaac Disraeli's village of Bradenham lies
near by up a side valley of the wide wind-gap that goes up to
Princes Risborough, and the quiet cottages lead up to the effective
climax of the church and Disraeli's Georgian manor house, all
backed by the long lines of hillside woodlands.

We regain the main road at the exquisite timbered and plastered
village of West Wycombe, with its forge, post-office and *Black Boy*
Inn now preserved in all their varied beauty for all time, owing to
the energies of the Society of Arts, a place of narrow passages,
overhanging gabled cottages and dogs sleeping in spite of the
traffic that unceasingly hurtles through.

Above the village, on a spur of the Chilterns, is a knoll studded
with junipers and yews, with a strange polygonal flint-walled
mausoleum and church with a massive ball on the top. This
church, which is only open on Wednesdays and Saturdays, has an
armchair instead of a pulpit. It was built in 1763 by Lord de
Despencer, and has a finely painted ceiling, and tomb of John
Dashwood and the builder. In the ball that surmounts the church
there is room for ten people. Despencer, better known as "Hell-
fire" Dashwood, had a reputation for wildness which it has been
suggested was exaggerated, though the actions of the Hell-fire
Club would seem to give the lie to that; the subject has received
full discussion in a recent book on the Club.

The Oxford road climbs up to the ridge of Stokenchurch, a
high lying centre of the chair-making industry. But there is
another quieter track which climbs up along Bledlow Ridge and
runs along a hog's back with wooded valleys on either side, that
used to pass, before it fell to pieces, a strangely attractive old
windmill with its works open like the inside of a giant clock. Just
ahead we are at Chinnor Hill on the edge of the Chiltern escarpment, a place of dramatic impressiveness with vast views over
the blue vale of Aylesbury and the plains of Oxfordshire. The
hill top is thick with beech clumps, and the sides of the steep
slopes well covered with ancient junipers and yews. Towards the
foot of this hill runs the ancient green track of the Icknield Way,
one of the oldest of the tribal routes. I turned along this track east-
bound, and was soon at partly suburbanised Princes Risborough
with its old market hall, where the Black Prince built a palace,
and Sir Peter Lely had his home. It is in a fine position where the
valley debouches on to the plain beneath the Whiteleaf cross cut
in the chalk, the subject of much speculation on its origin and

N

significance. Near above it is Rupert Brooke's *Pink and Lily*, probably the highest inn of the Chilterns, with immense views over the Vale all around.

Far more interesting is the less known Monk's Risborough, with a church of fine clerestories and a beautiful high timbered wagon roof. The rood screen has crudely painted panels of Charles the First's time. The near village is Great Kimble, famous as the place where John Hampden made his stand against ship-money; you can still see in the church a facsimile of the impost that Hampden refused to pay. Close by *The Barnard Arms* is the famous Elizabethan House of Chequers, bequeathed by Lord Lee of Fareham to all future Prime Ministers. It is a house of deep red brick and tall chimneys nestling under a high hill. Cromwell's great-grandson, Colonel Russell, preserved all the Protector's relics in this house.

The way from Chequers to Hampden is partly along a highroad, and then up a gentle slope over fields to the castellated two-storeyed Hampden House with a dry moat, and a white fence to keep the trespasser from straying on to a lawn on which grow two giant cedars. When I was last there, the house was shut up and there was no sound beyond the cawing of many rooks and the eerie screeching of peacocks on the lawn. The little church contains a flamboyant monument to a John Hampden, but the grave of the famous one remains unknown. In the large hall of this quiet house where Hampden was arrested are portraits of him, of his descendant Richard, who cut his throat here after losing his money in the "South Sea Bubble", of all the court beauties of Charles the Second's court painted by Lely, and of Elizabeth, Mary, Queen of Scots, and Mary of England. The Rector of Great Hampden, Robert Lenthall, lost his 15-year-old daughter, 21-year-old son, and his wife, all of whom died of plague in the month of August, 1647. There is a silver chalice in the hall containing the inscription "From this cup John Hampden received the Communion wine at the hands of Robert Lenthall, Rector of Hampden". Hampden was born in London in 1594, educated at Thame Grammar School, within a mile or two of the field where he was to receive his mortal wound, and Magdalen College, Oxford. In 1619 he married Eliabeth Symeon, who bore him nine children before dying in 1634. He became M.P. for Wendover, and his protest at Great Kimble against ship-money took place in January, 1635-6.

When Price Rupert appeared with 6,000 men at Stoke and had to retire to Brill, Hampden was one of his most active opponents. In 1643 he was fatally wounded at Chalgrove Field, and tried to reach his house where his second wife, Letitia Vachell, was waiting for him, but could only reach Thame where he died.

On the other side of the park there is a queer lane that leads to the tiny hamlet of Little Hampden, just a cluster of a few cottages, church with two-storey half-timbered porch and inn, *The Rising Sun*, overlooking a deep dell to a wooded ridge on the opposite side of the hill. Beyond Dunsmore lying in a dell is a lovely little inn, *The Leather Bottle* with a red and gold sign. Just ahead is Wendover, where Robert Louis Stevenson came on foot, knapsack on back, in 1875 and signed his name in the Visitors' Book of *The Red Lion* and wrote a fine panegyric of the low wainscoted parlour where he spent the evening. In the church, which has a fourteenth century tower rising above fine trees, are brass effigies to William Bradshawe, his wife, and nine children. The Christian names of twenty-three of their grandchildren are also given.

The place itself is a bright little town which has suffered from modern development, but retains some attraction; it is extraordinarily pleasantly situated on the Icknield Way with Boddington Hill, Bacombe Hill and Coombe Hill, at 853 ft. the highest Chiltern point, (67) all rising smoothly above it.

Aylesbury, proverbially famous for its ducks, though this is now questioned, is a happy-looking country town standing high above the green vale with a vast market place, winding ways and narrow passages. Round its market square are four fine inns, *The Bull's Head*, *The White Horse*, *The Crown* with an overhanging timber storey of Tudor and Jacobean work, and *The King's Head*, which was the guest house of a monastery and dates back to 1386. It has a fine stone gateway and a magnificent leaded wooden window with original heraldic glass with the arms of Prince Edward who was killed at Tewkesbury. Oliver Cromwell's chair is still shown, and also a priest's hiding place. This grand old inn now belongs to the People's Refreshment House Trust. The church stands in an even more charming square of solid Georgian houses and is remarkable for the spire which rises not from the ancient tower, but from a smaller lantern with an open parapet and slender pinnacles set astride the old tower's battlements. The ancient charnel house still stands below the Lady chapel, which is fourteenth century, and is now used as the crypt. There is also a fine Norman font. The vestry door, which dates from the thirteenth century, has an iron bar that is raised by a winch-key which passes into the middle of a boss and lifts the bar so that it swings into a catch on the jamb of the doorway. In this square is the old Grammar School, the Prebendal House, once the home of Sir John Wilkes, and picturesque almshouses with tall twisted chimneys.

Back in the hills we turn north again by way of the charming upland little village of The Lee which has a church with a well-designed fourteenth century piscina. A little to the north-east is Cholesbury, where stands a fine windmill. It is a place of much individuality, for the houses are set in a long line along a vast expanse of green common. There are traces of prehistoric fortifications enclosed by ramparts ten feet high with beech trees growing in the ditches protecting an ancient church which has been taken down and rebuilt.

On the same wide dry "wind-gap" valley which began at Wendover is Great Missenden on the Misbourne; it still retains a thirteenth century arch of its old abbey as well as a reconstructed fifteenth century roof of the monks' dormitory. The fourteenth century church which is well placed a good way up on a steep hillside slope has an impressive interior with a fine fourteenth century arcade of seven bays, and some quaint carvings. There is also a Norman font, and an immense seventeenth century monument to William Blois.

Little Missenden lies beautifully on the stream in a cup below the slopes of the Chilterns with its picturesque cottages round an Elizabethan manor house and a church which is very rich in mediaeval paintings. There are decorative paintings, one with the arms of Queen Elizabeth, a very early St. Christopher, ten feet high, brilliantly robed, and nine panels telling the story of St. Catherine. There is also a Norman font and a sturdy tower with mediaeval bells.

Further down the valley is the fine old market town of Amersham with an old street of black and white timbered and brick and plaster houses and water mills at either end. In the centre stands the fine seventeenth century market hall, open arcaded with a wooden louvre, an enclosed arch with a grille, peephole and metal bars behind which the local offenders were imprisoned. As a village town Amersham is quite charming and still remains unspoilt. The suburban and modernistic developments have fortunately so far stayed apart at Amersham-on-the-Hill nearer the railway.

Woodside Farm with its secret meeting-place of the Quakers was once the home of William Penn's bride, Guilelma Springett and on the way to Beaconsfield at Bury Farm we pass another home of the Springett family. In another of Amersham's old houses there is a very attractive group of wall paintings of the Nine Worthies, among them Julius Caesar, Joshua, David, Charlemagne and Godfrey de Bouillon, King of Jerusalem. The old timbered Grammar School is now used for other purposes, and there is a charming group of almshouses built by the Drakes of Shardeloes, whose monuments are to be found in the very interesting but painfully modernised church where John Knox declaimed against Mary Tudor and Richard Baxter argued with Cromwell's army. There are also interesting brasses of the fifteenth and sixteenth centuries. Nearby is the eighteenth century rectory where Henry Curwen lived and died. Shardeloes now a great classic house with its wide lake, standing in a hilly park of 700 acres, was once the place of William Tothill who had 33 children and in an earlier building entertained Queen Elizabeth. It has for very long been the seat of the Tyrwhitt Drakes and is a typical example of the earlier style of design of Robert and James Adam.

Just a little way up the hill is the hamlet of Coleshill with its fine windmill, once the home of the poet Edmund Waller. Some distance to the north of Amersham is Chesham with beechwoods standing above the little Valley of the Chess. It is from these beeches that all the wooden spades are made for children's buckets. In the river are the famous watercress beds of Waterside. The bustling little market town with its tanning and other industries has been pulled about and modernised, but a number of original houses help to retain some of its old character. The cruciform central-towered church stands at the end of a long avenue of 80 limes in a corner of the park overlooking the town. There is a cross here erected in memory of Thomas Harding, who was sentenced to wear a badge of green cloth embroidered with a faggot and later burned at the stake for reading Wycliffe's Bible. The transeptal church is thirteenth century with a Hertfordshire type lead spire added to the old central tower in the eighteenth century. In the Baptist chapel there is a record of one Thomas Sexton and his grandson who together preached in it for 111 years. Modern building has spread largely up the slopes and along the dry valleys that were cut by great prehistoric streams when the Chess was a mighty river.

But the most famous family hereabouts is that of the Russells of Chenies (68), a strikingly attractive village that has contrived to remain unspoilt in general effect, though the cottages are mostly of the model half-timber Victorian variety.

This village too is just above the tiny Chess, and has several pieces of little elm-shaded green, with a red-roofed well in the centre of one, and lawns sloping up to the fragment of the old brick Tudor manor house with its high pitched roof, fine gables and twisted chimneys, built by John Russell of Long Bredy, the Dorset farmer who founded the fortunes of the great house of the Dukes of Bedford, and married a Chenies heiress, Anne Sapcoate, in the sixteenth century. He lies in the church which has been quite excessively renewed and smartened up. The very resplendent Bedford chapel with its banners, magnificent marbles and black and white pavement is for some obscure reason locked from the public. It was built by Anne Sapcoate in 1556, and its seven monuments were described by Horace Walpole as "immense in marble, cherubim'd and seraphim'd". There are tombs in the chapel older than many to the Russells, notably one on which rests two fourteenth century members of the Chenies family.

There is a pleasant walk down the valley of this shallow crystal-clear stream past a ruined chapel to Latimer, which has a triangular green not unlike that at Chenies, a new red brick church by Sir Gilbert Scott and a fine brick Elizabethan house, now the home of Lord Chesham, but once the prison of Charles I and a sanctuary

for his son. At Flaunden close by is another early church design of
Scott's, with which we could readily dispense in favour of the
unique group which was wantonly destroyed to make way for
it,—an aisleless cruciform church and, closely attached, a two-
storeyed timber priest's house with turret.

South of Latimer lie the Chalfonts. Chalfont St. Giles is famous
for the "pretty box" which Thomas Ellwood found for his friend
Milton where he could write in peace, secure from the ravages of
the plague.

Of all the houses I know where famous men have lived, Cole-
ridge's at Nether Stowey, Wordsworth's at Grasmere, Burns's at
Kirk Alloway, and Dr. Johnson's at Lichfield, this lattice-
windowed, tall-chimneyed timber and brick cottage home of
Milton seems most successfully to have preserved the spiritual
essence of its most famous inhabitant. The garden is colourful and
quiet and an ancient vine still clings to its walls. It was here that
Ellwood made his famous remark: "Thou hast said much here of
Paradise Lost, but what hast thou to say of Paradise found?"
which gave Milton the idea of continuing his epic.

The square towered low-roofed church which stands above the
water-meadows has a picture gallery of considerable interest
including a painting of St. Anne, one of St. Catherine, and scenes
of the Expulsion from the Garden of Eden, which were there
centuries before Milton. There are many interesting brasses of
priests and knights. Here too lie the Fleetwood family who lived
at the Vache where Captain Cook once stayed with his friend
Palliser and out of compliment to him named an island Ile Vache.
In the park you will see the first monument ever erected to Cook,
on which is the inscription "the ablest and most renowned navi-
gator this or any other country has produced".

The next village of Chalfont St. Peter was the home of the
Penningtons, in whose family Thomas Ellwood was tutor. Sir
Isaac Pennington, Lord Mayor of London in Cromwell's time,
was arrested at the Restoration and died in the Tower, of which
he had once been Lieutenant. In the church, which is partly of
brick, there are two brasses to the Whappelodes taken over from
the older church. A long walk by the river and lake through the
fine grounds of Chalfont Park, after the war to be inconceivably
cut up by a London to Birmingham arterial highway which will
slash savagely across this Chalfont district, will bring us back
once more to Gerrard's Cross.

XV

THE SOUTH-WEST CHILTERNS

THE southern end of the Chiltern ridges is undoubtedly the finest
in scenery, and it still remains largely secluded and unspoilt.
From the wide "wind-gap" by Princes Risborough the steep
escarpment faces the vale of Aylesbury, densely and finely wooded
with beech. Behind this main stretch long wooded finger-like spur
ridges separate winding dry valleys running south-east towards
the Thames. Villages are few, small and scattered, and there are
some isolated hamlets in the valleys and on the upland commons.
There are glorious views over the vast plain, and on the southern
side close to such places as North End the clefts may be traced as
they converge towards Henley on Thames, with the faint blue-
grey line of the Berkshire Downs beyond. The London–Oxford
road from Henley by Nettlebed to Benson forms a dividing line,
and to the south, in the great bulge round which the Thames
curves, the character of the country alters,—the hills become
gentler and more undulating, while less cut up, and the whole
plateau-like landscape is on a smaller, milder scale, although the
abundance of the woodlands is no whit less. Hamlets are closer
set and there is more population, more evenly distributed. There
is a certain amount of building infiltration northward from Reading.

A good starting point for this south-west corner of the Chilterns
is Marlow, where is one of the most picturesque reaches of the
Thames, with the surrounding hills all covered with beeches.
Shelley, always impressionable to natural beauty, made a wise
choice when he settled in the red-tiled house in West Street to
write *The Revolt of Islam*, leaving his child-wife Mary to compose
her sole masterpiece *Frankenstein*.

The green is bordered by varied trees, but finest of all is the
sweeping curve of the wide river, with the graceful suspension
bridge composing with the church spire on the bankside.

A little further up the river we come at Medmenham to fragments of the Norman Abbey that was restored in the eighteenth
century by Sir Francis Dashwood, Chancellor of the Exchequer,
who held high revel here with his Hell Fire Club companions who,
calling themselves Franciscans, dressed up in blue and crimson
and held scandalous orgies. We have already heard of them at
West Wycombe (p. 89). Close by the river and church are a group
of picturesque cottages, a timbered fifteenth century manor house,
and a dormered sixteenth century inn, *The Dog and Duck*.

From here we follow the river a little way westward to Mill
End, where is Hambleden Lock with the old weatherboarded mill
house and its glazed louvre. We now follow for a very short
stretch the most delectable valley that leads to Hambleden, a place

of gabled houses, timbered cottages, and an old transeptal partly rebuilt church. Roman pottery and mosaic have been excavated at Yewdon Manor Farm.

There are good monuments to Henry Sandys, Ralph Scrope and Sir Cope Doyley, and three fifteenth century brasses. In the tower there is a fine piece of Renaissance carving which is supposed to be the end of a bed that once beloned to Cardinal Wolsey. In the churchyard is the grave of W. H. Smith who founded the famous firm of newsagents. The head of the family is now Lord Hambleden, and they have built a little museum for the Roman relics excavated from the large villas near by.

There is a pleasant walk north of Hambleden up the rest of the delightful stream valley among the folds of the Chilterns to Fingest, which possesses the most notable Norman parish church tower that I know. It is very massive with twin gables, or rather a rare double saddleback roof later in date. The tower is so massive that it looks as if it were originally built for defence. This aisleless twelfth–fourteenth century church is as good inside as out, for it has kept a surprisingly large proportion of the original fabric.

The church is surrounded by trees, and there is a cluster of cottages on two sides of it, and one Restoration red brick inn. This is a natural meeting place of dry valleys and wooded ridge-spurs, a nodal point which can afford an almost unending variety of rambles and wide-stretching views.

Near the head of the Hambleden Valley stands Turville (72), a lovely village with dormered and timbered cottages overlooking its little green, and a black capped windmill on the hill above, close to which is a ridge with flints arranged to form the words "Amici Mei".

The village is a quiet retreat of a few sawmills, an inn, *The Bull and Butcher*, and some unpretentious red-tiled timbered and brick cottages with dormer windows round a quiet green. Turville Park, built by William Perry, stands on high ground with splendid views over the wooded ridges.

The country now becomes unbelievably untenanted, for as we follow up the steeply ascending lane towards North End (through woods recently felled, alas) there is nothing in view but two bold ridges of beech woods with exquisitely symmetrical curved fields capping the long valley, a private place containing Wormsley, a big white Regency house, the seat of the Fane family, once the place of Scrope the regicide.

North End, at the top of this valley on the very crest of one of the long ridge spurs of the Chilterns, is a hamlet of great charm built along a green with two duck-ponds and tall trees with gorse and bracken covered expanses of common all over the place.

Soon we are at quiet pleasant little Christmas Common on the very edge of the escarpment looking down over red-roofed Watlington to the wooded vale that leads to Oxford.

68 A LANE IN THE CHESS VALLEY, NEAR CHENIES

69 FLOWERING CHERRY TREES IN THE CHILTERNS

70   REMENHAM CHURCH AND VILLAGE BY THE THAMES

71   THE RIVER CHESS, NEAR CHESHAM

There are many green tracks leading down the juniper covered slopes, perhaps the most inviting being that which crosses the Icknield Way just by the towers of Shirburn Castle, the home of the Earl of Macclesfield, which was held for the King in the Civil War until Fairfax took it in 1646.

It is well worth while turning south-west along that quiet green prehistoric track called by the country folk "the Hackney Way" or "the old Roman" that runs along the foot of the hill past the huddled streets of Watlington and the big Georgian red brick house of Britwell Salome, to the prettiest village of the Chilterns, Ewelme, The first building that strikes the eye is the tall fifteenth century two-storeyed red-brick school house. Then a narrow way leads up into a cloister, surrounded by brick and timber almshouses.

Quite close is the church, like the school and almshouses built by John de la Pole, Duke of Suffolk, of a great and tragic mediaeval family who were established at Wingfield in Suffolk. It is a fifteenth century building of very unusual beauty with mediaeval screens behind which is the rich and noble tomb of his wife, Chaucer's granddaughter, the Duchess of Suffolk who died in 1475, wearing the garter round her left arm. Her lovely effigy, and the grim 'skin and bone' version, the cadaver, below, are in this time of war both sandbagged. This Perpendicular church is in nearly every respect perfect, owing to Colonel Martin who was in command of the Roundheads here in the Civil War and protected it, even to the extent of warning his troops that if they entered the church it would be over his dead body. There is a magnificently carved wooden canopy above the octagonal font. Only some yellow-painted Gothick pewing inserted by a saintly vicar about 1833 strikes a jarring note.

Outside the church the main attraction of the village is the clear stream that runs for a mile by the side of the road, widening to the King's Pool and shortening again to fall over in a cascade, broadening out into bunches of watercress beds.

Among many brick or white-washed thatched and tiled ancient cottages there are unfortunately some garish new ones covered with advertisements in tin. It is an idyllic spot, but at the time of writing no one in it will give you tea; for that you must be prepared to bus or trudge it down to Benson by the river.

Even in this brief cursory sketch it is hoped that it may have been established that this end of the Chilterns possesses noble woodland landscapes, and is an extremely remunerative and satisfying district for any kind of rambler. It is still comparatively unknown and little visited, but is threatened by building development from Wycombe and Reading, and it is hoped that some of its loveliest spots may be preserved for ever in the London Green Belt.

O

XVI

HERTFORDSHIRE : BERKHAMSTED TO BISHOP'S STORTFORD

In many ways the crowning glory of the North Chilterns is that series of three cone-shaped peaks that stand above the little hamlet of Ivinghoe, and one of which, the Beacon Hill, takes its name from that village (74). This is very reminiscent of the South Downs in its smoothness, the softness of its turf and the vast extent of its views. It has one added advantage; to the south is a glorious woodland of beeches and bracken and giant box-trees, known as Ivinghoe Common, which belongs to the National Trust, who also own much of the splendid six miles hill-top expanse of Berkhamsted Common—a fine range of gorse and bracken, woodland, glades of beech, hawthorn, birch and other trees, strangely and romantically preserved against the spoliation of enclosure just over a century ago.

At Ringshall is one of the grey lodge gates leading to Ashridge Park, where the Bonar Law Memorial College now occupies the site of the house founded by Henry III's brother as a Convent of the Order of Bonhommes. "A pleasanter place than Ashridge is, harde were to finde, as Skelton rehearseth with words few and playn". Queen Elizabeth was staying at Ashridge when she was arrested by Mary for complicity in Wyatt's Rebellion. The house has twice been rebuilt since her time, once in 1606, and again on a much enlarged scale in revival Gothick between 1808–14 by Wyatt, completed by his nephew who did so much at Windsor.

The tall monument with a green ball on the top that stands at the end of an avenue a mile and a half long commemorates the third Duke of Bridgewater, the father of British Canals. Disappointed in love by the lovely heiress who jilted him, he went north to occupy himself with his coal mine at Worsley, and finding the freightage by road to Manchester too costly, arranged with Brindley to cut a canal to the Mersey. This exploit was so successful that he was soon making a profit of £80,000 a year, and extended his scheme to other inland waterways, which until the coming of the railways were able to carry all heavy goods at a cost infinitesimal compared with the roads. Many tales are told of his eccentricities.

At the edge of Ashridge Park, which covers a thousand acres and has many splendid trees, such as the famous Frithsden beeches and Queen Anne's lime walk, is the straggling but picturesque village of Little Gaddesden, with a Perpendicular church restored by Earl Brownlow in 1877. At Great Gaddesden is the L-shaped

72   TURVILLE VILLAGE IN THE CHILTERNS, FROM THE SLOPES OF ITS HILL

73   A SUDDEN DIP IN A CHILTERN ROAD

74. WINGLOE BEACON AND WINDMILL

house of Sir Walter Halsey, which was built in revived classic style by Wyatt in 1774, in a large park with fine views of the surrounding woods. Gaddesden Row has some quiet cottages set back pleasantly across wide grass verges.

But the most attractive village near here is Aldbury, where the cottages are grouped round a large green with pond, above which is an enormous elm by the old stocks and whipping post, which have survived the brutal treatment of a gang of hooligan visitors. The restored church is Early English and Decorated, with an exceptionally tall western tower, a Verney Chapel and fine stone effigy of Sir Robert Whittingham, who was Privy Councillor to Henry VI and was killed at Tewkesbury. I watched the interesting ceremony of loaves being distributed to the poor after Sunday meetings in this church, by order of the Harcourt Charity of 1721. There are particularly pleasing almshouses of thatch, weather-boarding, brick, tile and plaster, which are familiar to many people owing to the popularity of Aldbury among artists. What I like best about the village is the way that it conforms to the curves that lead to the wooded slopes just above. It nestles most comfortably in its quiet niche. Mrs. Humphry Ward, the Victorian novelist, lived at a house called "Stocks", and described the place in *Bessie Costrell*.

On the other side of Berkhamsted Common, lying on the main line of the L.M.S.R. and the Grand Junction Canal is Great Berkhamsted, famous as the birthplace of William Cowper, and for its Public School, originally founded in 1541 and reconstructed 300 years later. Berkhamsted, which has been a good deal rebuilt and has a fringe of suburbanisation, is a warm comfortable-looking town of red brick with a main artery that is part of the old Akeman Street, containing many picturesque houses and inns and a much restored cruciform church with a central tower 100 ft. high, and a much ruined castle of many historic associations, which was taken by Prince Louis of France in 1216. It is now well tended by the Office of Works. It was once the home of the Kings of Mercia, and later of Thomas à Becket. Chaucer was Clerk of the Works here.

Among other notable buildings is the sixteenth century timbered Incent House, the home of the John Incent who founded the Grammar School, which is a fine building of old brick with mullioned windows and a handsome hall with open timber roof.

The central towered transeptal church is one of the largest in Hertfordshire, and possesses massive arcades of the fourteenth century, as well as a later screen with modern figures on the panels. There are interesting fourteenth century monuments to Richard and Margaret Torrington (1356), a tablet to Cowper's revered mother, an altar tomb to John Sayer, who was Charles II's chief cook, and there are a number of good brasses, notably one to John Raven, Esquire to the Black Prince.

Not far from Berkhamsted is Hemel Hempstead (Hamelame-stead of the Saxons) largely and unattractively extended and modernised, with a High Street that rises over the shoulder of a cliff that leads down to the River Gade, famous for its mills in Saxon days and its eels when Domesday Book was compiled. Its great attraction is the fine unspoilt Norman church with a tall leaded spire added in the thirteenth century to the central tower, and chevron-patterned Norman arches. On the north side of the twelfth century vaulted chancel is a very picturesque passage with narrow doorways and arches.

At Apsley End there is a paper mill that supplied the Government with the paper for our early postage stamps. One of its owners, Dickinson, discovered how to make paper in a continuous roll, which made possible the enormous editions of newspapers. One of the partners in this mill was Sir John Evans who acquired fame also as an archaeologist; he specialised in early flint implements, and his children have also accomplished much sterling research.

One of the most interesting cities in Britain lies not far to the south-east, St. Albans, which takes its name from the first saint in England to die for Christianity. It was here that the Wars of the Roses began; it was here that King Offa of Mercia built the little Saxon church that grew into the present vast cathedral. Long before the Romans came to found Verulamium there was a prehistoric settlement near in Prae Wood.

Offa founded in 793 a Benedictine Abbey to commemorate St. Alban, in atonement for his murder of Ethelbert. This abbey was rebuilt by the Normans and among its forty abbots was Cardinal Wolsey. Of that Abbey only the church and the magnificent fourteenth century gatehouse remain.

It is the second longest cathedral in the country and stands high; consequently its tower, which is 144 ft. high, is a landmark for miles around, though standing apart from the little town on rather lower ground.

The gatehouse, which is of three storeys, was built in 1363, and was used as a prison for French soldiers in the Napoleonic wars. For the last seventy years it has housed the boys of the school,—who for long were accommodated in the Lady Chapel, up to 1870,—which goes back nearly a thousand years and boasts among its scholars Sir John Mandeville the mediaeval traveller, Francis Bacon and his father Sir Nicholas. The gatehouse was besieged in 1381 by a mob of rioters led by John Ball.

In a city so old and so new we expect to find a strange jumble of architecture. The Clock Tower in the High Street, now used (in peace time) as a museum, built in the fifteenth century, has a curfew bell cast in 1400, which used to summon apprentices to work at four in the morning, and sounded at eight at night to close the shops and market. Near the tower is the narrow French

Row, so called from the French troops who occupied it in 1216; we have heard of them at Berkhamsted. Particularly striking is the tile-roofed *Fleur-de-lys* Inn with overhanging eaves.

Two battles of the Wars of the Roses were fought in St. Peter's Street, and in the Lady Chapel of the Cathedral lie the bodies of the Earl of Northumberland, the Duke of Somerset and Lord Clifford, who fell in those battles.

In Dagnal Street is the old Moot Hall with a timbered storey overhanging one of W. H. Smith's shops. But the most attractive range of gabled and plastered houses is in Fishpool Street on the way out of the town.

On the way to the site of Verulamium, going down Abbey Mill Lane, where silk is still made in the mill, we come to a tiny whitewashed octagonal house with one very tall white chimney. This is *The Fighting Cocks*, of mediaeval date, one of the oldest houses in the city, but not one of the oldest inns, because it only became a hostelry in the sixteenth century.

The first thing we notice about the long cathedral is the West Front which, like some others, was unhappily rebuilt in the last century by Lord Grimthorpe; he devoted much misspent attention to tinkering and falsifying at a cost of £140,000. The cathedral itself is built in the form of a cross, 550 ft. long and 177 ft. across the transepts. The walls of flint, brick and stone include much taken from the Roman city. Its interior contains, with later Decorated additions, a good deal of its original Norman work, which is remarkable more than anything for its bare simplicity. One of its finest features is the magnificent stone reredos with replaced statues behind the altar which dates from 1484. There are the remains of painted reredoses, notably one of the Crucifixion, against some of the nave piers, where there were undoubtedly former altars. The roof is finely embossed and retains much of its old colouring. There are two fine chantries, of John of Wheathampstead and Robert Ramryge, both very richly decorated. In the Saint's Chapel still stands the pedestal on which St. Alban's shrine rested, with its broken tracery very carefully and successfully pieced together. Above it is the fifteenth century wooden watching chamber, where sat a monk always on guard to see that no harm befell the shrine. There is also a rare grille of Sussex iron, forged in 1275 and painted blue and gold. Here is the two-storeyed monument to the good Duke Humphrey of Gloucester, who gave the first books to found a library in Oxford. There are also a number of interesting mediaeval brasses.

After the Cathedral it is worth paying a visit to the Museum in the Clock Tower, that is particularly rich in local antiquities from prehistoric and Roman days. One of the three tenth century churches stands near the museum. This is St. Peter's, badly over-restored some time ago; it has a massive tower, some old glass and a bust of Edward Strong who was Sir Christopher Wren's master-mason. The next tenth century church is St. Stephen's, which has a shingled tower and spire, a porch of stone and timber, and in the churchyard with its hawthorn avenues is a Roman milestone. The chancel arch is of oak and the fifteenth century brass lectern is supposed to have come from Holyrood, buried in the Civil War and recovered in the eighteenth century. The last of the tenth century churches, St. Michael's, is inside the boundary of the Roman city and occupies the site of the Forum.

There are still traces of the Saxon wall and a good deal of Norman work, and even a blocked doorway of Roman brick, also three particularly fine brasses. It is in this church that Francis Bacon was buried, and from the lodge-gates near by is a fine drive leading to the roofless walls of his old house of Gorhambury. The new house close by, which has an impressive eighteenth century portico of ten Corinthian columns, with some fine interiors, was built in 1778 by Lord Grimston and is the country seat of Lord Verulam; it was possibly designed by Wyatt.

The Roman city of Verulamium has recently been magnificently excavated through the enterprise of Doctor Mortimer Wheeler and his band of helpers. Here was established in A.D. 45 the first Roman city, covering about 150 acres, the only British town to hold the rank of municipium, in which the people had the rights of Roman citizenship.

In A.D. 61 Boadicea, in her fury with the people for submitting to the Romans, attacked and destroyed it in the absence of the Governor. The second Roman city was built in the second century, and the third and final city, built in the shape of a rough oval, covered 200 acres, enclosed by two miles of massive walls of flint, with towers and four gateways. It possesses the only Roman theatre yet excavated in this country, a mosaic pavement in black, grey, ochre, white, pink and red, and more tesselated pavements housed in the very complete museum, coins, jewels, ornaments, weapons and the footmarks of men and animals. The foundations of the London gate show it had two roadways for wheeled traffic and two for pedestrians, a hundred feet broad.

We are not far from Wheathampstead, with its memories of Charles Lamb, who talks, in *My Relations*, of going in search of cousins "through the green plains of pleasant Hertfordshire". In *Dream Children* he writes lovingly of Blakesware, where his grandmother, Mary Field, was housekeeper, and of Mackery End, where Bridget and Elia made an excursion "to beat up the quarters of some of our less-known relations in that fine corn country".

"The oldest thing I remember," he says, "is Mackery End: or Mackeree End, as it is spelt, perhaps more properly, in some old maps of Hertfordshire: a farm house, delightfully situated within a gentle walk from Wheathampstead. . . . By somewhat a circuitous route, taking the noble park at Luton in our way from St. Albans, we arrived at the spot of our anxious curiosity about

75   SUMMER-HOUSES BY THE RIVER LEA, WARE, HERTFORDSHIRE

76 A CHAPLET OF COWS BY WIDFORD CHURCH, HERTFORDSHIRE

77 GEORGIAN HOUSES BY THE CHURCH, HATFIELD

noon. The sight of the old farm house, tho' every trace of it was effaced from my recollections, affected me with a pleasure which I had not experienced for many a year." What a poignant picture he gives us of Bridget traversing "every outpost of the old mansion to the wood-house, the orchard, the place where the pigeon house had stood (house and birds were alike flown), with a breathless impatience of recognition".

I, too, know Mackery End well, and have pleasant memories of "those pretty pastoral walks" that lead to it, and of tea on the lawn in front of the happy-looking warm red brick house, now much restored. It has two Dutch gables, tall twisted chimneys, a central clock tower, fine rectangular windows and a noble porch. It once belonged to my friend Apsley Cherry Garrard, the owner of Lamer Park, who went out to the South Pole with Scott and gave a most moving account of the trials of that brave venture in *The Worst Journey in the World*.

Nearby is the strangely remote hamlet of Ayot St. Lawrence with its interesting ruined medieval church with still erect tower, and its Georgian successor designed in 1778 by Nicholas Revett, author, with James Stuart, of *The Antiquities of Athens*, with a classical portico and side colonnades, that stands some way from the road near a Tudor manor house (p. 111). At the end of the colonnades are small buildings with memorials to Sir Lionel and Lady Lyde who built it, and to the architect. This church has a coffered ceiling, and its details are carried out in delicate Greek design; the old church still retains a fifteenth century tomb of a knight and his lady. Bernard Shaw lives in the vicarage of this quiet village. There is also in this Ayot a square dovecot of very unusual attraction with vertical timbered sides.

South-east lies Hatfield, the home of the Cecils. The great house was built by Sir Robert Cecil, son of the Lord Burghley, Queen Elizabeth's famous Counsellor. Sir Robert died before he was able to live in it.

The town is quite delightful with its picturesque cottages and Georgian houses running steeply up from the little *Eight Bells* Inn, (77) to the church set high on a lawn among fine trees with a timber house at one corner of it, and eight gates of wrought Sussex iron that once encircled St. Paul's, of which we heard at Lamberhurst in Kent.

And the loveliest of all is the old mellow brick palace with its tower gate-porch, once owned by the Bishops of Ely. Of this palace there remains a fifteenth century archway with a fine mullioned window and heavily buttressed west front with a square tower, and a stepped gable crowned by a twisted chimney. The great hall, which for long was used as the stables, still retains the magnificent timbered roof and the solar still stands. It was here that all three of Henry VIII's children spent their earliest years,—Elizabeth was here when Mary came to the throne, and she was here once again when the news came that her sister was dead and she was queen. The last charger of the Duke of Wellington lies buried nearby.

Close by, overshadowing all, is the great house that Robert Cecil built on Elizabeth's death, shaped like an E, nearly 100 yds. long with two vast wings enclosing a great courtyard. It took four years to build and cost £40,000. It now presents a most imposing array of towers and domes and windows. The south porch, dated 1611, is an Early Renaissance "frontispiece"; it rises to a great height with three tiers of fluted columns, and behind is the clock tower with an open lantern above it. The great hall has two screened and panelled walls and two covered with tapestries.

But perhaps its crowning glory is in the main staircase with richly carved newel posts with cupids. There is a two-storeyed chapel with arcaded galleries and panelled walls, and there are two galleries that run from end to end of the main building. The lower one is known as the Armoury and the upper as the Long Gallery, with a richly decorated ceiling and fine panelling. Among the treasures of the house is the death-warrant of Mary Queen of Scots, Lord Burghley's diary, the Council Book of Mary Tudor and several relics of Queen Elizabeth.

The park, which occupies about two square miles, has the River Lea flowing through it, and is seven miles round its great brick walls. There is a statue of the late Lord Salisbury in front of the gates leading to the Great North Road. He is buried in the church, where there is a bronze by Goscombe John. Here too is a twelfth century knight, and the handsome tomb of the first Earl, who built the house; his effigy is supported on a dark slab by four graceful kneeling female figures of white marble with a skeleton between them. It is a striking early piece of English baroque design.

The Salisbury chapel has delicate Renaissance screens and marble wainscoting on the walls. Lord Melbourne and his wife Lady Caroline Lamb, who became infatuated with Byron, both lie here, and there is a window in memory of Lord Balfour's mother. In the south or Brockett chapel among many monuments, is the canopied tomb of Sir John Brockett with his helmet on the wall The Reaves and Brocketts lived in the solid red eighteenth century house known as Brocket Hall which passed out of their hands to the Lambs and so to Lord Melbourne. It has many excellent late Georgian interiors and a fine ironwork staircase. The present owner has taken his title from the name of the house.

The church which houses all these ornaments is one of the largest in Hertfordshire and has a massive tower which was built in the fifteenth century, crowned with the usual little Hertfordshire spire. There are Jacobean altar rails, a fine piece of embroidery said to be the work of Queen Elizabeth, silver candlesticks and an altar cloth that was part of the pall at George III's funeral.

From a Drawing by J. C. Buckler

78   THE VILLAGE OF KIMPTON, HERTFORDSHIRE, A HUNDRED YEARS AGO

From a Drawing by J. C. Buckler. ca. 1835

79 ANSTEY CHURCH, HERTFORDSHIRE, FROM THE NORTH-WEST

80 ASHWELL, HERTFORDSHIRE

From Hatfield the obvious direction to take is that over the quiet countryside that leads to Hertford. The capital of the county stands on three rivers, with an ancient castle which was once the home of Saxon Kings. It was the meeting place of the first National Assembly ever held by the Church in this country; the second was held at Hatfield, which we have just left. Soon after the Danes came and burned the castle down. It was rebuilt by Alfred's son Edward, and then came the Normans to build once more the walls that still remain.

Here Queen Isabella lived and died, and in 1356 the Black Prince brought King John of France to be a prisoner. It was here that Bolingbroke drew up his indictment of Richard II. There are many sterling timbered and pargeted plaster houses, particularly in St. Andrew Street and Honey Lane—mixed up with many that are anything but picturesque.

Lombard House, overlooking the River Lea, is one of the most attractive with its wooden mullions, overhanging storey and five gables, once the home of Sir Henry Chauncy, a seventeenth century judge who in 1712 declared Jane Wenham of Walkern to be a witch. She was the last woman sentenced for witchcraft in England and after her reprieve by Queen Anne witchcraft was deleted from the Statute Book, though not from the beliefs of many of the people. It is good to know that she was provided for by Col. John Plumer of Gilston. The seventeenth century grammar school stands just by the church of All Saints. But Hertford's most famous school is the Christ's Hospital School for Girls, a very attractive group of buildings, approached by a shady avenue, set up in 1683, with coloured figures of Bluecoat boys and girls set about the walls. The eighteenth century Shire Hall was built by the Adam Brothers, but looks gloomy in its amorphous brick; in it hang the portraits of Hertfordshire worthies including C. J. Fox.

Now brought into the outer area of the town itself is the curiously-named hamlet of Bengeo (pronounced Bengy) where the little-used unaisled church of St. Leonard retains its original Norman apse. Near also is the trim village of Hertingfordbury on the Mimram or Maran; at Cole Green, not far off, is Earl Cowper's seat of Panshanger, where a pseudo-Gothick house is surrounded by justly-famed gardens of great beauty.

Another house in the Hertford area is Balls Park, belonging to the Faudel-Phillips family. Its plain symmetrical exterior covers an exceptionally interesting series of mid-seventeenth century interiors, wood-panelled and with modelled plaster ceilings, transitional between Jacobean and Later Renaissance design.

Another attractive village on the river Lea with large estates is Essendon, boldly placed on a jutting spur above the river valley; it has a church with a fine cedar standing in the middle of the village. The estates are Bedwell Park, with a collection of old

P

masters that is open to the public, and Essendon Place, the home of Lord Dimsdale.

Everybody knows that there is a great bed of Ware, and that John Gilpin lived there, but I have met few people who have ever been to the place. Yet the Danes brought their ships up the River Lea to this point, and in the fourteenth century Ware was a most important town.

It is now a pleasing quiet place of red roofs with a grey church with a little Hertfordshire needle that stands finely up among gardens. It is the chief Hertfordshire centre of malting, and has massed brigades of cowls, but perhaps the most attractive feature are the overhanging summer-houses and old brick garden walls seen across the Lea (75). Gilpin House and *The Johnny Gilpin* remind us of Gilpin's association with the town, and the Bluecoat School, built in 1686, was the school used by Christ's Hospital until it moved to Hertford in 1760. There is a good deal of fourteenth and fifteenth century work in the cruciform church of St. Mary, notably a carved oak screen, vestry doorway, a nave roof which is particularly handsome, and octagonal font, well carved with saint figures.

It was at Ware Park that the great bed of Ware was originally housed. It is 11 ft. square and 7 ft. high and is very richly carved. After being transferred to *The Crown* Inn and later to *The Saracen's Head*, it later went to Rye House, and now rests in the Victoria and Albert Museum, where sightseers have side bets on the number of occupants it will comfortably hold.

On the eastern border of the county is Bishop's Stortford, mainly notable as the birthplace of Cecil Rhodes. The town is attractively set on a hill, but is rather slummy around the maltings by the station. The outer walls and moats of the Norman Waytemore Castle can still be traced, and two of the ancient inns, the plastered *Boar's Head* and timbered *Black Lion*, still carry on their trade. The modern church of All Saints, in spite of its fine rose window, is overshadowed by the fifteenth century church of St. Michael's with its pinnacled tower and spire standing proudly on the top of the hill. It has an imposing arcade of six bays, and richly carved choir stalls with misericords, which are supposed to have come from old St. Paul's. Among notable monuments are those of Lady Margaret Denny, (1648) Maid of Honour to Queen Elizabeth, George Jackson, who befriended Captain Cook, Thomas Dimsdale, the doctor who inoculated Catherine of Russia for smallpox, for which he received a fee of £10,000 and an allowance of £500 a year, Sir George Duckett, improver of Stort Navigation, and Francis Rhodes the vicar, whose son was the famous Cecil Rhodes. The pleasant three-storeyed whitewashed house in which Cecil Rhodes was born is now a Rhodes Museum. The old Grammar School where he was educated is now the parish hall.

XVII

CENTRAL AND NORTH HERTFORDSHIRE

WE are now in an almost unknown chalk upland country of smooth swelling gentle hills and shallow winding dry depressions with an occasional small stream, little coppices and enormous parks.

Kimpton is a typical village of this neighbourhood with its large white plastered farms strung out along a curving highway and a thirteenth century church with the typical county lead spire set upon a knoll embowered with trees (78); it was much altered in the fifteenth century and includes two notable medieval oak screens, one of which has a vaulted canopy. Here rest the 24th Lord Dacre and second Lord Hampton, who lived at The Hoo, which is surrounded by a fine park of 250 acres. The timbered and plastered houses of the village are well spaced out below the church and the rising ground above. It is approached by a quiet and most attractive avenue.

At St. Paul's Walden, near its twin hamlet of Whitwell (which has a village hall with a timbered storey), is a church approached along a grand avenue of tall trees with a remarkable Georgian chancel with a semi-circular panelled Palladian ceiling and chancel arch filled with an eighteenth century classical screen. The gates of the screen are usually locked but it is possible to climb through the openings.

The pleasant quiet Adam house with twin bays of St. Paul's Walden Bury is the home of Lord and Lady Strathmore and the birthplace on the 4th August 1900 of our Queen.

In the area that is bounded by Luton on the west, Stevenage on the east, Hitchin on the north and Harpenden on the south is a very pleasant quiet stretch of small-scale upland country with little hamlets called "Ends" and "greens", quite distinct from the villages. Tea Green, Mangrove Green and Perry Green have not only fascinating names, but are fascinating in their complete seclusion. The largest of them, Breachwood Green has been, however, horribly spoilt.

On the north-western edge of this territory is the rim of the chalk escarpment where stands Lilley with wide views over the flat sparsely wooded Bedfordshire clay plain.

Here are memories of Rupert Brooke who used to walk this country when he was an undergraduate at Cambridge, along

"The Roman road to Wendover
By Tring and Lilley Hoo."

The Docwra family once lived in the great park of Putteridge Bury nearby, and in the church, which has linenfold panels and a

Norman chancel arch, the two famous sons, John and James, of the seventeenth century curate Janeway were baptised. James almost rivalled Bunyan as a writer of moral books for children. John was a mystically inclined divine of particular sweetness of character, who died very young.

Close by is Hitchin, a typical small market town of great antiquity which still retains many of its old houses and little closes and alleys. Mr. G. T. Hine, a solicitor of the town, has written in two volumes a very able and full history of the town, as well as a separate contribution on nature, prehistory, etc.

One of England's smallest rivers, the Hiz, which is only a few miles long, flows past the church which is the largest in Hertfordshire, and has a massive but low tower with a big stair turret, lovely canopied mediaeval font, a wooden fifteenth century screen, elaborate and fine, and magnificent porch with niches filled with statues. Most of the roof is fifteenth century and there are many good brasses. One of the marble monuments is believed to represent Bernard Balliol, the great grandfather of the founder of Balliol College.

Close by the church and the river are the Biggin almshouses, with a courtyard surrounded by a walk with timber pillars.

Eugene Aram was a schoolmaster at Church House, and George Chapman, the translator of Homer, was born at Mount Pleasant in 1559.

The Icknield Way runs below the escarpment here; above Hexton it becomes remarkably impressive, with a large camp, Ravensburgh Castle, on a boldly projecting spur point from which there is a grand view of the wide vale and surrounding country, a very outstanding lookout point.

Only a short distance along the Icknield Way is Baldock on the other branch of the Great North Road, with an exceptionally wide street of old houses and jolly inns, more or less unspoilt, but with an unexpectedly incongruous modern stocking-factory at one end, mercifully apart from the village buildings.

The church is a large fourteenth century building with a big tower crowned with a lantern spire, three fifteenth century screens the whole width of the church, a staircase door to the priest's room, several brasses and a memorial to John Smith, one time rector, who as an undergraduate spent 10,000 hours deciphering the 3,000 pages of Pepys' diary without the key that Pepys himself had left in the library of Magdalene, Cambridge.

Letchworth, earliest of garden cities (dating from 1905), is in the open fields on the other side of the Great North Road. It is well laid out round the old Manor House and owes its inception to Ebenezer Howard who developed a site of 5,000 acres, which gave the lead to Welwyn and Wythenshave. It is curious that side by side with this city lies the site of a British settlement that was inhabited as long before Christ as we live after His birth.

There is however a third Letchworth with a timbered post-office with dormer windows, a seventeenth century Hall and a little church with old benches and brasses, and a stone figure of one of the Montfichets whose name is recalled by the village of Stansted Mountfitchet on the way to Cambridge.

A little way down from the Icknield Way is the ancient large village of Ashwell with an old trackway of its own known as Ashwell Street. It is particularly attractive and unspoilt and has a large range of houses big and small of good craftmanship and design. The great church is impressive with its big gaunt thirteenth century tower with needle spirelet (80), mediaeval screen and fine tracery in the east window. It is remarkable for its 'graffite' which include a drawing of old St. Paul's and a sentence in Latin about the visitation of the plague "Miserable, wild, and distracted, the dregs of the people alone survive to witness: and in the end a tempest".

Ashwell, set as it is in a countryside of open fields looking over Cambridgeshire, is attractively placed as well as being attractive in itself. Below the road is the river Rhee, a tributary of the Cam and the many ash trees are said to account for the village's name.

Still walking north-east along the grain of the hills we come to Roe Green, where the cottages are placed round the edges of an enormous green, but the church is at Sandon, a little way off. It is a fourteenth century building with a fine brass dated 1480 of FitzGeffrey, a simple fifteenth century screen, and Jacobean carved pulpit.

The twin villages of Kelshall and Therfield are right on the escarpment edge, where it projects boldly outward and provide views of exceptional width over the flat, almost treeless plains of Cambridgeshire.

In the fifteenth century church of St. Faith Kelshall which has a flat painted roof and is very light and cheerful, we again have a memory of the pietistic John Janeway of whom we heard at Lilley. His father was rector here, and here he was laid to rest in 1657, carried off by consumption when only 23 years old.

Therfield, high on the last spur of the Chilterns, is tucked away protectingly under roofs of thatch.

Barkway, on one of the roads to Cambridge, has some very fine gabled plaster houses and others have steeply pitched roofs of thatch. One house in the main street belongs to the National Trust; there are several inns that were once posting houses.

But the finest church in the district is that of Anstey, that lies off the high road and is approached by a good thrice divided timber lychgate. It is of good proportions, mainly fourteenth century and has a central tower and transepts, the former surmounted by a Hertfordshire needle (79).

Still a little to the north-east we come to a small area where Hertfordshire, Cambridgeshire and Essex are all mixed up, with the highest point in all East Anglia at Langley Upper Green which stands 480 ft. up. In this area among the uplands Heydon, Elmdon (82), Chrishall, and Great and Little Chishill are all interesting and some are dowered with vast edge views.

The country here, largely arable, is moulded in sweeping downland curves with lonely sheepfolds and isolated haystacks (12, 81, 91). To the east is the north-west Essex country to which we shall return later.

Facing south once more we have the Pelhams, Brent, Furneaux and Stocking. At Brent Pelham we can still see the tomb of Piers Shonks, the dragon slayer of 1086 in the wall of the church, which has the usual spirelet and small graceful tower. Furneaux Pelham Hall is a sterling brick building of that interesting transitional period of 1640–50 with curved gables and some interior panelling.

Westward we pass the Hormeads, one of which has some splendid iron scroll work on the door which dates from the late twelfth or early thirteenth century (8), and contrasts admirably with Thomas de Leighton's later work at Eaton Bray, not far away in Bedfordshire, with a similar example at Leighton Buzzard. He was the smith who forged the Eleanor grille in Westminster Abbey.

And so we come to Buntingford with its pleasant wide street, once a Roman way, terminus of its own little branch line of railway. The houses are full of fascination with their deep archways, red and yellow roofs, gables and overhanging storeys. There are seventeenth century almshouses grouped round a flower filled courtyard, founded by that doughty old theological controversialist Doctor Seth Ward who used to walk over from Aspenden every day to the free school till he left for Cambridge.

Here he lost his fellowship by refusing to take the Covenant, and became Professor of Astronomy at Oxford before being appointed Bishop, first of Exeter, then of Salisbury and second president of the Royal Society.

Close to the almshouses is a seventeenth century red brick chapel of ease to Layston where St. Bartholomew's was the mother church of Buntingford. It is of flint and was long a ruin, but has now been restored; the village of Layston has now completely disappeared.

In the main street are many old houses jumbled together and a number of signs hanging from fine ironwork.

The next station down the line is Westmill, a village in the shallow Rib valley which roused the Hon. Humphrey Pakington to almost rhapsodical eulogy.

It has a charming green, a range of plastered dwellings and a thatched cottage at Cherry's Green called Button Snap which belonged to Charles Lamb though he never lived in it. In *Elia* we hear of the pride of ownership that swept over him as he paced over his "allotment of three quarters of an acre with its commodious mansion in the midst, with the feeling of an English freeholder that all betwixt sky and centre was my own."

One of the curates, Nathaniel Salmon, after submitting to William III, refused to take the oath of allegiance to Queen Anne, irrationally enough, as she was a genuine Stuart. A gifted and versatile creature, after resigning and refusing a good Suffolk living, he practised as a doctor and wrote voluminous histories of Hertfordshire and Essex, and caustically of the Restoration Bishops.

At Westmillbury is a thatched mediaeval barn, one of the four early examples in the county; its roof timbers rise from the ground and its bays are of the traditional 16-feet width.

To the west is a very secluded district of high lying cornfields and lonely little villages, but near Aston is Astonbury a 1630–1640 tall narrow brick house with fine moulded brick chimney stacks, four front and two end gables, all curved, and twin square staircases in big rectangular projections. They are of different Jacobean design, but both of carved newel, drops and turned baluster type.

And this brings us back to the Hertford–Welwyn line.

Drawn by F. L. B. Griggs, R.A.
AYOT ST. LAWRENCE'S CLASSIC CHURCH (*v. page* 103)

XVIII

HERTFORDSHIRE: THE EASTERN BORDER

JUST south of Bishop's Stortford is Thorley, where the church has a Romanesque south doorway with twisted shafts and bold chevron arches, and rood stairs with the top door intact. One of the rectors here was Samuel Horsley, the eccentric scientist who conducted a controversy with Joseph Priestley for twelve years, and attacked Sir Joseph Banks at the Royal Society; he believed that Napoleon would set up as Messiah. Thorley Hall is moated and dates from the sixteenth century.

At Sawbridgeworth on the Stort and the Cambridge main line are still many old cottages of timbered and plastered brick in Bell Street, though the picturesque malting figured in the County *Highways and Byways* has alas vanished. The church has a sturdy tower with the usual county flèche, and a vividly coloured stair turret of red brick adjoining. The massive south door is of original oak backed by a square framework.

Nearby is Hunsdon, famous for the house which Henry VIII acquired for his children from Sir John Oldhall. There have been changes since Elizabeth gave the house to her cousin Sir Henry Carey, Lord Hunsdon, whose family chapel in the transitional-Perpendicular church has a fine Jacobean screen and contains the great monument in alabaster of his son, Governor of Berwick-on-Tweed for the Queen.

At Gilston on the Stort we once more have memories of Charles Lamb, for it was here that the Plumer family lived who are described by him in his essay on "Blakesmoor-in-H—shire". It was one of the Plumers who befriended Jane Wenham of Walkern and gave her a cottage after she had been acquitted of witchcraft. In the church, which stands in the Great Park, are monuments to the Gores, who after the Chauncys lived in the great house before the Plumers.

Close by Hoddesdon, where the shade of Izaak Walton hovers very near, fishing-rod in hand, coming up from the Lea looking, alas, in vain for his favourite *Thatched House*, though many of its other inns that he must have known remain unchanged.

The river Lea, so beloved of Walton, fills the moat of what is left of the Rye House, the Tudor brick gatehouse where the Rye House plot to assassinate Charles II and James Duke of York on their return from Newmarket in 1683 was hatched. It was here that William Penn's wife Gulielma died. Further down the river Lea stands Broxbourne, a place of many rivers and streams, winding and intersecting, which in spite of many new buildings still keeps its old church, oak panelled priest's house and giant yew.

Another place that reminds us of Izaak Walton is Amwell,

81   A WINDING UNFENCED LANE IN THE CHALK COUNTRY NEAR ELMDON, NORTH-WEST ESSEX

82 ELMDON VILLAGE, NORTH-WEST ESSEX

83 A WINTRY EVENING AT THE BELL INN, BENNINGTON, HERTFORDSHIRE

where that "pack of otter-dogs of noble in sadlers" met in the early morning and aroused such lyric enthusiasm in Venator. "Look, down at the bottom of the hill there, in that meadow chequered with water-lilies and lady-smocks: there you may see what work they make: look! look! you may see all busy! men and dogs: dogs and men: all busy."

It was Hugh Myddelton, the London goldsmith friend of Sir Walter Raleigh, who ruined himself in making in 1609–13 a new river for London by turning the waters round Amwell and Chadwell into a 40 mile long channel to empty themselves into the Islington reservoir. There is a monument to him on the tiny island made by the divided waters, with verses by John Scott, the local Quaker poet, whose grotto survives at Ware. It is a graceful Adam urn, one of the few cases in which a memorial is noble in itself and not merely commendable for its associations.

Close by is the public school of Haileybury, originally designed by Wilkins, architect of the National Gallery, for the East India Company, where Sir John Lawrence and Sir Henry Outram were educated, first of a great line of eminent soldiers brought up here.

At the south-east corner of the county is Cheshunt, greatly overbuilt and suburbanised yet with much of interest, for one of its gateways is the Old Temple Bar, and the hall of Wolsey's old home still stands. There is a particularly fine Perpendicular church, and on its outskirts is the famous Waltham Cross, richest of all the twelve crosses set up to mark the places where the body of Queen Eleanor rested on its way to Westminster. Old Temple Bar, which was designed by Sir Christopher Wren, was bought by Sir Henry Meux and is mercifully preserved by being set up in 1888 as one of the gateways to his house in Theobald's Park, no thanks to the Corporation of London. Charles I grew up here, and went out in 1642 to raise his standard in Nottingham, and outside this wall Oliver Cromwell's son Richard (Tumbledown Dick) dragged out a weary old age in lodgings for which he paid 10s. a week.

Cardinal Wolsey lived at Cheshunt Great House, now owned by the Freemasons, where we may still see the panelled hall with its fine fifteenth century timber roof and a fragment of the moat.

Over the highlying common of Goff's Oak with its derelict windmill and fine views we come to Cheshunt Church, which was built in 1420 by Nicholas Dixon, its rector for thirty years (1418–1448) and has a huge ironbound coffer and many memorials and gravestones of interest.

South of the Lea Valley, where it curves round in its great angle from east by north to flow due north-south, is a secluded stretch of wooded upland country, still very sparsely settled, and as attractive as it is little known (86). It is really part of the old Enfield Chase and a northern stretch of the Forest of Middlesex, originally connected with Epping Forest, and like it containing

Q

many hornbeams, whose bleached "key" seed vessels and pale yellow leaves often persist into winter. This fine forest stretch has been mercifully preserved by its incorporation into great private parks, whose owners have stoutly resisted any attempts at building exploitation, the threat of which hovers near from the L.N.E.R. loop line which cuts through the middle of the district. This railway track was constructed as an alternative to avoid the great Welwyn viaduct over the wide Mimram valley, which takes only one single line, and after sweeping over the river valley at Hertford rejoins the original line at Stevenage. There has been a great deal of suburban development round Crews Hill, and the quite considerable settlement at Cuffley among the neighbouring large glass-house ranges has spread up to the fine slopes of Great Wood, but beyond the unattractive highlying hamlet of Newgate Street towards Bayford are the great woodlands, cut up by green rides into a sort of chequer-work of oak, ash, birch, hornbeam and hawthorn, with often dense undergrowth and gnat-haunted in late summer. The meandering lanes have often wide grass verges, and an occasional weatherboarded cottage pair forms the only habitation. One road of this type runs from Tyler's Green to the Lea at Broxbourne (86), and when in the last war parties of the Middlesex Volunteer Regiment used to tramp to Nazeing for trench digging, they could count the five-mile stretch by a house a mile; since then this way has, I hear, been attacked by bungalows. It is to be hoped that this forest woodland area will be preserved by eventual incorporation in the London Green Belt; its destruction would be an irreparable loss, infinitely to be deplored.

A little north-east of Potter's Bar is Northaw, another Hertfordshire village beloved of Charles Lamb, who used to climb up here from the wooded valleys of the Lea and Colne. Here he refreshed himself with ale in a back parlour before losing his way on the heath at Little Berkhamsted. James I acquired part of Northaw Common for his estate at Theobald's Park. It is still sequestered, or was recently, and its rather humble cottages, diversified by one or two moderate-sized Georgian houses, are compactly placed round the prominent well-proportioned modern church. There are still pleasant hilly lanes with green margins to repay aimless rambling, unless they have been lately bungalow-beset. An obelisk stands at Cuffley to remind us of William Leefe Robinson's memorable feat in bringing down the first Zeppelin in England in 1916. A year later another Zeppelin was shot down in flames close by, between Northaw and Potter's Bar; I believe no monument is raised to its fall save the English oak on which it was impaled in a ruined pyramid of shattered metal fragments. The memorials to the unknown dead of both crews lie in a semi-circle of some fifty unnamed headstones with Luftkapitän Mathay in the centre. Will the Germans, one wonders, hold services in their memory after the present war, when so many

84 AN ARABLE STRETCH IN SOUTHERN HERTFORDSHIRE

85   A SNOWY SCENE NEAR CUFFLEY, HERTFORDSHIRE

86   WINTER SUNSHINE NEAR WORMLEY ON THE WOODLAND WAY FROM
HATFIELD TO BROXBOURNE, HERTFORDSHIRE

more German airmen have met their last end above English soil
and sea?

North Mimms has one of the best smaller village churches in
Hertfordshire (p. 75), almost entirely of simple but effective Decorated
design, with a rich west doorway figuring in Rickman's and
Brandon's *Gothic Architecture*. Its rather large needle spire is of
copper, green in colour, and it is full of interesitng memorials.
The church stands in the park, not far from the fine Jacobean
red-brick house which was built by Sir Ralph Coningsby in 1602.
There are three other parks in the parish—Gobions, now a
Regency house which replaced the old building where Sir Thomas
More used to stay, Potterels, and Brookmans Park, now a trans-
mitting station whence wireless messages radiate through the
ether above the site where the great and munificent Lord Somers,
Baron Evesham, pored over his literary collections two and half
centuries ago. The curious Tudoresque red-brick "folly" gateway, tall and scraggy, is rather uncertain in date, but most probably
of the eighteenth century.

Under the ridge in a retired spot is Salisbury Hall, a fine house of
the Restoration, at the end of a lonely lane, but I have not found
out much about it. It may be compared with Tyttenhanger not
very far away, a red-brick house of the later seventeenth century
with projecting side wings and a central glazed turret. It possesses
one of those finely carved scroll staircases which I always find
particularly attractive; there are others at Dunster Castle, Tythrop
in Oxfordshire. Eltham Lodge, Kent, and, as we have seen, at
Guildford (p. 17).

But the walk by Ridge Hill is the most agreeable country stroll
near the Metropolis; I have known country-lovers pent in the
town on urgent tasks come all across the city for its healing and
refreshment. You walk from a ruined farmhouse and good barn-
yard across the level upland stretch; in front the ground drops
sharply to the wide expanse of the fields and woods of southern
Hertfordshire, with the strong square abbey tower of St. Albans
a dark note in the nearer distance. The scene is wide and fair, but
on the other side is for a bit a gently sloping countryside stretching
to Barnet ridge with its church tower. Soon however, your way is
backed by woods and an occasional pond—what matter if the
copses are wired off; we know we owe their presence to the land-
owners, and they are ours for the looking, with bluebell glades in
spring following on windflower patches as delicate as any Kent
can show. So we circumstroll our little ridgetop oasis and make
our way back by some track or other to the high roads at South
Mimms with their ceaseless roar of whirring traffic.

XIX

UP AND DOWN WEST AND NORTH-WEST ESSEX

LONDON's main lung to the east is of course Epping Forest which is much less well known and visited than it deserves to be, owing to the depressing miles of mean streets that have to be passed before you reach the magnificent ancient forest that runs for some eleven miles northwards from Leytonstone to Epping. It is part of the ancient royal hunting ground of Waltham forest, and fallow deer and roe deer are still to be seen flitting among these thick and many-branched hornbeams.

In the heart of the woodland are the two ancient camps of Loughton and Ambresbury, the latter being traditionally known as the fortress which Boadicea held against Suetonius. A good many relics of the Bronze Age have been unearthed here.

The fact that this fine land of heath and woodland and undulating hills has been kept free from the builder is due to the foresight of the Corporation of the City of London who after a stern battle lasting for three years managed to acquire these 5,500 acres for the use of the public for ever at a cost of £250,000.

Down in the valley to the west lies Waltham Abbey, an ancient market town with a church bequeathed by Edward the Confessor to Harold, who is said to have been buried there. It was converted by Henry II into an Abbey in 1172 and became the richest in Essex until Henry VIII seized it in 1540. Its remains were restored in Victoria's reign and the church still retains seven bays of the old Norman nave, its western tower built in 1556, and a Norman doorway and font.

All roads out of London to Essex are purgatorial at the start, though not nearly so penitentially or so protractedly as the railways, which is why it is far preferable to take a motor coach than a train. The most pleasant route is that through Epping Forest, which can be joined at say Chingford by a connecting link with one of the new by-passes. The stretch through the Forest is nearly free from bricks and mortar, and has a restful appeal under any weather conditions, and Epping is definitely a bright little country town (with the huge burnt shell of ruined Copped Hall away to the left) for all the blatancy of its red brick water-tower. We fork right just beyond the town end, for though the highway to Cambridge by Bishop's Stortford which sticks close to the rail is not without pleasant points, with a gem at Newport, the parallel way by Dunmow goes deeper into more rural Essex.

Immediately to the east a stretch of barish upland lies to the north of the last detached pieces of Epping Forest, between that little town and Ongar, with the log nave of the little Saxon church of Greenstead-juxta-Ongar (p. 78) among enormous aerodromes. It is early eleventh century and in all probability was built as a chapel for the body of St. Edmund on its journey from London to St. Edmundsbury in 1013. North is the Roding country, as remote and bucolic as ever, though scarcely now to be described as "the land of windmills." It is not specially featureful, but has a sense of restful peace, and its cottages and farms have a stamp of sterling genuine East Anglican craftsmanship. Further south, Abridge, a bus terminus well within the London area, leads in a short way to two remarkable houses: Albyns, a solid pile of 1630-ish brick-work, with a carved staircase and many plaster ceilings and panelled rooms painted white with stars; some years ago the panelling was torn out, to be sold across the Atlantic it is said. The other mansion, Hill Hall, is a rather later and larger house of brick with stone pilasters, an abundance of interiors with rich plaster ceilings, and elaborately laid-out gardens in which an array of huge Venetian water-jars was prominent. But the place has changed hands several times recently.

This area, threaded by the little sluggish unpretentious river Roding which finds its way down to the Thames at noisome Barking Creek, has the cluster of eight Roding villages* dotted across it intermixed with the two smaller groups of the Easters and the Lavers, mostly with small unpretentious churches, though High Easter has a dignified building of some size with a tall brick tower, near an attractive half-timber inn disfigured by advertise-ment signs. Not far to the east and north is the weirdly named hamlet of Shellow Bowells, and the two little churches of Wil-lingale Doe and Willingale Spain in the same churchyard (88), and Pleshey with its memories of John of Gaunt and the Shake-spearean sketch of its decrepitude in *Richard II*. Only a few over-grown fragments of masonry and a high grassy bank remain. It is this quiet countryside that has called forth the deep affection of the poet Arthur Shirley Cripps, missionary in Mashonaland, whose yearning verses written on a south-bound liner have found their way into anthologies.

The road to the west of the Roding country, with its few habitations and view of Great Canfield church on the slopes above its stream, leads to Great Dunmow, a typical clean bright little Essex market town, full of attractive houses. It is at Little Dun-mow that the farcical revived flitch ceremonies are held, and here is a fine building, turned into cottages, with the early type of single-storey central hall, now very decrepit. Felstead is an excel-lent village, and the school has some old buildings, while little Leighs Priory is one of the Great Tudor halls of Essex, lonely in a low situation. To the north-east however, as we shall see on

* White, Abbess, Berners, Leaden, High, Aythorpe, Beauchamp, Margaret Roding.

our return way lies the country of the "fields" in the Pant valley, secluded and charming above any in East Anglia, and comparable with any area in England for those who like quiet pastoral landscapes.

In what does the charm of the Pant valley country with its 'field' villages consist? It rather defies analysis, and the impressions made on different observers will vary materially, but it has a suave graciousness that is yet far removed from lush softness, a beauty of subtly modelled landscape and human craftsmanship superadded that recalls a piece of Georgian silver, the bright tenderness of a suite by Rameau. The little quiet river with its fringing willows is apostrophised by the Hon. Humphrey Pakington in his *English Villages and Hamlets* for the fundamental unsuitability of its name; in March, however, it can rush along in deep and tearing spate, so that a detour of three or four miles is a small price to pay to avoid fording one of its many watersplashes. The river itself has a course which is as short as it is normally peaceful; rising in the upland area of Wimbish not far from Saffron Walden it is engulfed in the Blackwater at Bocking hard by Braintree. Those of us, however, who love both stream and surroundings maintain stoutly that the course below Braintree past Witham to the sea at Maldon *is* the Pant, and the stream which wanders in like a flattened S-shape from Coggeshall is merely a parvenu tributary. It was thus in ancient times, for the Saxon battle *Song of Maldon* refers to 'Pante'. From any highlying point near Blackmore End there is a view over the middle section of the area, where the spectator seems to stand near the rim of a shallow bowl, while all round spreads the well-cultivated landscape, which could be shown to any visitor from overseas as typically English in its quiet well-ordered yet unsophisticated harmony. At one house the people find that visitors from London are still often obsessed by the age-old myth that Essex is flat. Any person volunteering this statement is sent for a good round cycle-ride, and in every case, however strong and experienced as a cyclist, it is invariably found that he has frequently had to dismount to climb the short sharp hills. But the works of man here provide no anticlimax; even the humble labourers' cottages are of unaffected craftsmanship; the farms attain even nobility, and there are Tudor manors, Georgian rectories and residences, as well as a slight sprinkling of Victorian red brick. The churches are many of them excellent; Finchingfield has much of interest from several periods.

We come to Finchingfield from the south by way of a gentle slope past a series of greens leading to the river and pond which are crossed by a little crooked brick bridge that swerves off modestly to the left to give an unimpaired view of the red-roofed whitewashed cottages that rise in tiers embowered with trees leading up to the grey towered church on the further knoll. The

88 THE CHURCHES OF WILLINGALE SPAIN AND WILLIN-
    GALE DOE, ESSEX, IN THEIR COMMON CHURCHYARD

87 THE INTERIOR OF THAXTED CHURCH, ESSEX,
    LOOKING EAST

89   QUIET COUNTRY BETWEEN ASHEN AND CLARE, ESSEX AND SUFFOLK BORDERS

roads all fall into the cup of the main village green with a noble sweep before being gathered together to join the one winding main street. The pool is guarded by picturesque white posts which add greatly to its charm.

Finchingfield's main claim on the eye is that it seems to have been composed for its portrait with the perfect art that conceals art, for all its lines are harmonious. There is neither discord nor confusion anywhere and yet it must have achieved its artistic co-herence quite naturally. The church is of flint with a fine Norman doorway and imposing screen. It contains a monument to William Kemp of Spains Hall (now the home of the Ruggles-Brise family) who kept voluntary silence for seven years because he had unjustly accused his wife; his monument is drawn here.

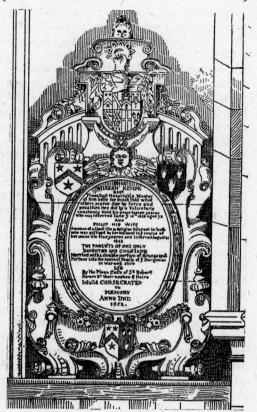

Drawn by F. Chancellor, F.R.I.B.A.

WILLIAM KEMP'S MEMORIAL TABLET,
FINCHINGFIELD CHURCH

His ill-advised remorseful self-sacrifice may have hastened the passing of his young wife, who died in 1623, in the fifth year of his vow. But his self-imposed silence was destined to have further tragic consequences later in the same year. Riding home with a groom one evening Kemp was caught in a storm of great vio-lence and the pair sheltered in an old ruin, where they overheard a gang of desperadoes plotting to rob his own home of Spains Hall. On the way home they found the ford over the Blackwater deep in a rushing flood. Kemp wrote a brief note to prepare the house-hold, and the groom struggled through the deep running water, while he went round a longer and safer way. But on arrival at the house the message had been so soaked as to be utterly illegible. The faithful household retainers thought it best to sally forth armed to meet and protect their master. They thus left the house

unguarded and open to the attack of the robbers, who had forded
the swollen river shortly after. They seized everything of value
they could carry away, and murdered a boy of some seven years,
a distant connection of the Kemps; they left no trace or clue and
were never discovered. Kemp was finally persuaded to resume
ordinary human intercourse by Stephen Marshall, a gifted young
preacher of Wethersfield whom he had presented to the living of
Finchingfield. He lived another three years after he resumed normal
speech and attendance at worship, dying in 1628 at the age of 73.

Shalford, with bold arcade of fine proportions that suggests the
masons of Thaxted, has a series of remarkable tombs; if its aspect
is a little unkempt and forlorn it has at least escaped the hellish
horrors of Victorian bedizenment. But it is in the villages that the
local building attains its highest point; Panfield, Wethersfield, the
Bardfields, Great and Little, and, as we have seen, above all
Finchingfield, to which two little Victorian monograph books of
great interest have been devoted. All of them have their white
plaster houses of unaffected well-proportioned design, with
church and an occasional larger house, Tudor or Georgian; at
Gosfield is a long low Henry VIII House. To the east the undulating stretches shelve rather sharply to the Colne Valley, with a
wide view over miles of hedge-timbering across the slopes to the
gentle heights on the other side which separate it from the Stour
Valley (89), with a glimpse as you plunge downward of Sible
Hedingham church in a lonely upland situation, miles seemingly
from its village. With this solitary retired church is connected one
of the most romantic of the English adventurers in Europe, whose
colourful stories do not seem to have been collected as they might
into a volume which would make all fiction seem tame and dull.
John Hawkwood was the son of a Sible Hedingham tanner, and
left his London tailor's apprenticeship to serve abroad in Edward
III's wars. A Knighthood for bravery at Poitiers launched him on
a career in Italy as military adventurer, and after rendering high
service to the Pope, he married the niece of the Duke of Milan
and died wealthy and distinguished at 70. It is considered that a
canopy in the church is of his tomb, where his body was brought
to lie. Not far away is Stambourne, where Charles Haddon Spurgeon
the magnetic popular Victorian preacher was born, and of which
he has left so racy a description: "Let him mentally put together
certain up and down roads, with broad margins of green and walls
of hedge; ponds with ducks and goslings, *ad lib.*; plots of woodland; fields of turnips, oats and barley; a windmill; two or three
nice houses, with gardens and lawns; numbers of cottages which
could hardly be more picturesque; great wealth of fine trees;
stretches of meadow land; valleys and undulations; pigs and
donkeys; and withal, a general disorderliness of fertility, and a
sense of being out of the world, and of having nothing particular
to do, and you are getting an idea of Stambourne".

90   THE WAY INTO SAFFRON WALDEN, ESSEX

91   A DOWNLAND LANDSCAPE BETWEEN HEYDON AND GREAT CHISHILL, NORTH-WEST ESSEX

Past Tilbury-juxta-Clare with a little primitive church, and the quiet hamlet of Ashen, a mile or two of tree-shaded lanes leads across the upper Stour into Suffolk and the pleasant delights of Clare (89). But we must look at Little Maplestead, at once the smallest and most countrified of English round churches—though it belonged to the Knights Hospitallers and not the Knights Templars,—and Castle Hedingham, where on very private ground is the great Norman keep which shares with Rochester the supreme grandeur of this early castle form. Every one in Castle Hedingham particularly maintains that Shakespeare's

Drawn by M. and C. H. B. Quennell

THE KEEP, CASTLE HEDINGHAM
(WITH FOREBUILDING RESTORED)

plays were written by the Earl of Oxford, whose ancient stronghold rises so majestically above the surrounding landscape.

This keep is 110 ft. high, 62 ft. long and 55 ft. wide with walls of flint 12 ft. thick. It was founded by Aubrey de Vere about 1,100 and Stephen's Queen Maud died here. The castle was dismantled in 1592 and its parks broken up by the seventeenth Earl who was a notorious spendthrift. But if the castle can only be admired afar off, there is much to enjoy in the large and compact village of brick and half-timber, while the church in its proportions and stateliness would achieve distinction in any county, with its noble brick tower, varying Transitional arcades and some wonderful tombs, one of black marble. There is fine timber in the *Wheatsheaf* and *Old Falcon* inns and the Little Lodge farmhouse.

The country to the north, i.e. due E. of Saffron Walden to the Cambridgeshire border, is barer and less wooded, a plateau region in fact, which just at the Cambridgeshire line reaches over 400 ft. and gives that physically low county its only little bits coloured pink on the Bartholomew half-inch map. In certain states of the season or weather or of the visitor's mood and temperament it may appear gaunt and bleak; it can be very lonely (91), with its widely scattered hamlets, and occasionally you can find secluded a finely-timbered fifteenth century Tudor farmhouse such as that owned by the writer Hector Bolitho. Ashdon is a particularly attractive village with a half-timber guildhall by the churchyard and a room completely painted in seventeenth century strapwork in panels at the *Rose and Crown*, whose landlord has or had the strange Surrey name of Enticknap. At Hempstead, a naïf little place, is pointed out the little plastered inn where Dick Turpin was born, and where, when as a boy gone to bed upstairs, he would put his eye and ear to a hole in the floor and was fired to the highwayman's profession by what he heard of the adventures of the knights of the road. A curious little circular enclosure just opposite with a fringe of willows around is called Dick Turpin's bowling green. Over towards the Cambridgeshire border by the infant Granta is Hadstock, lonely in the great fields with a completely unrestored church of haggard grace where the door was once covered with human skin—it is said of a sacrilegious Dane. The door has been removed but a part of the wood is still preserved. But if this arable chalk upland, with its wide sweeping undulations and scattered patches of trees etched against the sky line (12, 81, 91), can sometimes have an unexplained charm, and sometimes fail to attract, there is always a thrill in the view of the wide and almost treeless plains of Cambridgeshire from the more definite escarpment to the west of Saffron Walden through Heydon, Elmdon, and in the Royston district Therfield and Kelshall, in an area we have already traversed.

Thaxted is one of those almost perfect little village towns which find their most typical and refined development in East Anglia. There is not much of the outlying hamlet of Cutlers Green, which seems to point to its metal-working manufacture in the middle ages. The row of thatched almshouses leads to the church, one of the great imposing parish fabrics of England (87). There is a connection with Edward III, and the great building is of the finest period of Decorated, noble in its design and gracious in proportion, with transepts, fine tower and crocketed spire rising to 181 ft. (one of the few stone spires in Essex) and a later Perpendicular chapel. The late Vicar, Conrad Noel, has done a great deal to preserve and restore this beautiful fabric. It stands on the top of the sharp knoll and at the bottom of the slope is the Guildhall with its open arches and the half-timber recently re-exposed by the removal of the seventeenth century plaster panels; on the eaves are still preserved the long hooks to tear the burning thatch from the roofs, when Thacksted, the thatched place, was a more exact description than at present. From the Guildhall runs an island of half-timber buildings, crowded and picturesque, and in the main street there are plaster Georgian fronts which show in their carved brackets and moulded beams that the eighteenth century has but lightly overlaid the fifteenth.

Up to the outbreak of war a local firm ran a coach service from

92   ST. MARGARET'S CHURCH, MARGARETTING, ESSEX

93   THE GREEN, WRITTLE, NEAR CHELMSFORD

94   FARMCARTS IN AN ESSEX BARN

95   THE BLACKWATER AND ST. MARY'S CHURCH, MALDON, ESSEX

King's Cross to Clare via Thaxted, and on a summer evening just before harvest to run through the undulating unspoilt countryside, with wide fields of corn and grass meadows was to savour the material expression of those qualities of orderly grace, of active and busy peace, of gracious simplicity, which have gone for a thousand years to the making of these most typical of English pastoral landscapes, have served to maintain them in the face of all changes in conditions, difficulties of indifference and neglect, and are now applied with a calm yet stubborn determination in their defence and martial upholding. Near Thaxted is the moderate-sized but fine Tudor house of Horham Hall with its noble brickwork, great traceried high bay window and panelled great hall, though a heavy hand laid upon it a huge tower-like addition in the 1850's. In spite of this its gables, turrets, parapets and high chimneys make a most picturesque display.

Saffron Walden, Thaxted's neighbouring cousin, is a larger town in itself and has increased by the growth of residential outskirts of suburban type, though its position on a loop of road and rail from the main Cambridge route has saved it from ruthless transforming modernisation, and enabled it to keep a good deal of its original Tudor character. But it is, and always has been, more accessible than Thaxted, and hence has kept a trading activity denied to the other on the extinction of its industries at the close of the mediaeval period. I shall always have an affection for it as the first country town I reached on an unplanned exploring ramble, cycling off one Sunday afternoon aimlessly from Hampstead and, finding myself there unexpectedly, decided to pass the night in the town. The place is built on gentle swells of land, has an abundance of old houses of varied character covering three centuries, and a church as large and imposing as Thaxted, and like it placed on a culminating high point. But its later erection has caused it to be throughout of fully developed Perpendicular without any reminiscence of Decorated, and the effect though light and airy has a touch of chill regularity about it. The tower and spire are an extremely successful effort of Thomas Rickaman about 1825. There is a marble tomb to Thomas Lord Audley who died in 1544. In the market square with its touches of spaciousness *The Rose and Crown* inn, though a good deal altered, stands out for its Restoration character, and further on is the row with coarse vigorous pargetting, where Cromwell may have stayed, and of which the house with the great figures was once *The Sun Inn*. But at the crest of the rise, as a lane leads right, up to the church, is on the little recess to the left an adorable group of Tudor building with a half-timber malting frequent in East Anglia. As the way drops down out of the town it passes by a jumble of old street houses as full of charm as anything in East Anglia (90), reminiscent of Fishpool Street, St. Albans, but surpassing it, as it does also that much be-photographed street in Warwick. But Saffron

Walden has much else that is individual—a turf maze cut on the common, and as uncertain in date and origin as most of these productions, a little "Old Dutch" garden which, if it is a modern production, has somehow caught the character and some of the spirit of the historic formal gardens. The Museum is a model of a small town institution in attraction, interest and arrangement—there are chalk mantelpieces, old fireplace implements, and especially a fine collection of Tudor diapered wall paintings preserved from regrettably demolished country houses and farms. A black vase of Roman (Samian) ware shows a female figure modelled with exquisite grace, drawn by a crowd of winged phallic emblems.

Round about this district the signposts (when not taken down) have a pleasant custom of specifying a place passed on the way as well as the destination: "To Walden by Arkesden". The country round the town is of unusual attraction: It is the hilliest chalk stretch in Essex, with fairly deep-cut valleys and fine large timber in the abundant woodlands. Near the main road is the great park and house of Audley End, which cost £190,000 to build, of Early Renaissance style with fine interiors, in the present state of which the hand of the Victorian decorator has probably had something to do. This great house, described by Evelyn as "one of the stateliest palaces in the Kingdom . . . a mixed fabric, twixt antique and modern" was also characterised by James I as "too much for a King, but it might do very well for a Lord Treasurer". There were originally two vast quadrangles, of which the larger was 205 ft. each way with four circular towers, and behind stood the smaller, of which three sides remain and form the present house. It was built between 1603 and 1616. It was sold by the third Earl of Suffolk to Charles II, but it reverted to the Suffolk family before being sold in 1747 to the Countess of Portsmouth who reduced it to its present size.

In 1784 it was acquired by Lord Braybrooke who spent £100,000 on restoring it. The great hall which is 90 ft. long has a finely carved Jacobean screen. There is a famous library of 8,000 volumes and a fine collection of Holbeins, Knellers and Lelys. The Tudor brick stables and almshouses are of good proportions and craftsmanship. The portions of the building demolished are preserved to us in the engravings of that remarkable and original character, Henry Winstanley, of the neighbouring village of Littlebury, maker of curious hydraulic devices, and designer of the extraordinary Heath-Robinson first Eddystone lighthouse, on which he perished in the great storm of 1703. His village of Littlebury is full of well-built old houses and is a compact little place clustered round its church. His well-designed house (now vanished) was shown to visitors for years after his death. A mile or two to the west lies Strethall, in a country bare in effect in spite of its occasionally extensive woods, little more than a small primitive church, of which part may quite well be Saxon.

To the west lies the diamond of hilly country between Walden, Royston, Buntingford and Baldock, where Essex, Cambridgeshire and Hertfordshire are very much mixed up, with Bedfordshire taking a stretch not far off; it is remote and secluded, though fairly thickly besprinkled with villages and hamlets, and crossed by two main north roads and the S.W.–N.E. line of the modernised Icknield Way. There is much that is of interest in this area, but it has had, as it deserves, a separate account. We have seen that particularly among churches Anstey and Ashwell would adorn any area, even the Victorian-ecclesiologist-worshipped Northamptonshire, and the latter is set in a village which takes high rank among those of all England.

We have now with many side diversions rambled up from town to the north edge of the county at Saffron Walden and back to Braintree by the Pant valley and the "Field" village country. Local twentieth century industrialisation contrasts with the remains of fifteenth century manufacturing at Coggeshall on the way to Colchester, a fine old wool village town which refused the railway some century ago and has in "Paycockes" an ideal wool merchant's dwelling which can rank with its stone counterpart, Wm. Grevel's house at Chipping Campden, though the rich carving of its front contrasts with the austerity of Cotswold stone. Paycockes has many brick chimney pieces and panelled interiors and has been carefully though perhaps somewhat excessively restored; as it belongs to the National Trust it is accessible two or three days a week.

We will keep W. and N. of the great and ancient London–Ipswich highway, the main way into East Anglia for many centuries; the stretch to the East will repay a separate exploration. There is Faulkbourne, a large brick fifteenth century mansion of Tudor type, very strictly guarded by its owners. But we ought before to have tried to track down that house at Feering which had so charming a panelled room illustrated in Hall's *Baronial Halls*, but it looks as if it had vanished for good. Witham on the main line and rail is remarkably unspoilt, with its excellent street of varied houses, if we disregard the ceaseless spate of traffic that whirls through it. Up above the important railway junction is the attractive little hamlet of Chipping Hill which Beckett suggests may be the original market meeting-place. There is not a great deal to stay for in Chelmsford, on which the bishop's seat presumably now confers city rank. The Cathedral has been so much pulled about and rebuilt that its tower and East Anglican flint porch are the only old major features which contribute to its dignity. The town can now be by-passed.

Writtle, close at hand, has a pleasant village green (93); around are scattered churches which exhibit the mediaeval Essex craftsman's handiness in timber and brick.

Margaretting has a fine timber tower, south aisle and chapel of brick (92), Jesse east window of original brick and many other features of interest in spite of the brutality of its 1870 restoration. Ingatestone is the original seat of the ancient Catholic family of Petre. In the church are memorials to many of the family, including Sir William who accommodated his religious convictions to suit Henry VIII, Edward VI, Mary and Elizabeth, and died in 1572, John, first Lord Petre (1613) and his thirteen children, and another to William who was privy councillor to four sovereigns.

Ingatestone Hall was built by Sir William in 1565, and was originally a quadrangular building of brick, but it is now the home of poor Catholics, and the Petres live at Thorndon. Miss Braddon laid the scene of *Lady Audley's Secret* at Ingatestone.

Modern additions to this village have effectually and finally robbed it of its charm. Doddinghurst has a timber weatherboarded tower in diminishing stages, like Blackmore, with shingled spire, and timber porches, which are found of such fine design at Margaretting—largely renewed. At Shenfield the fifteenth century arcades are wholly of timber and there is a tall slender shingled spire. Havering-atte-Bower with cottages sprinkled sparsely round its wide up-country green is surprisingly and delightfully rural considering its nearness to the huge brewery town of Romford which has expanded enormously to the south since the last war. Chigwell and Chigwell Row are still in pleasant country, and *The King's Head* is a fine large inn, rather smartened up, which appears in Dickens's *Barnaby Rudge* under the name of "The Maypole". Past Hainault Forest, a sorry piece of Victorian meddlesome destructiveness where some belated efforts have been started to do a little towards repairing the mischief, stretch the miles of Victorian and twentieth century suburbs, where the cutting of a tube railway will, with the electrification of the main line, do much to relieve an appalling congestion of communications, but may result after the war in the final disappearance of what pieces of rural country remain within reach of the line, in a spate of new suburban building.

96   A MILL ON THE CREEK NEAR THE CHURCH, BRIGHTLINGSEA, ESSEX

97　THE BARGE "RESOLUTE" TACKING ON THE STOUR ESTUARY ON ITS
WAY WITH FREIGHT TO MISTLEY

XX

EAST AND NORTH-EAST ESSEX FROM THE THAMES TO THE STOUR

THE Thames marshes are usually supposed to be the last word in monotonous dreariness, and yet explorers of Essex who have left this southern edge to the last have been struck by its bright fresh greenness and cheerful rural air. There are features of interest on the way from London to Southend, which was originally only the hamlet of South End in the parish of Prittlewell, with its fine chequer pattern church,—a mere cluster of fishermen's huts. At Belhus Park by Aveley is the earliest domestic essay in Gothick of the eighteenth century, (*ca.* 1733) and by no means unsuccessful at that. But a place of exceptional interest and attraction on this route is the Laindon Hills, where a bold knoll rises to 386 ft. above the undulating green plain. The village of Laindon lies far to the north and there is a little hamlet here, of a few houses and an inn, with another called *The Fortune of War* at a cross roads towards the river, named it is suggested after Sir John Hawkwood, who held land locally and had as we have seen at Sible Hedingham in the north-west of the county a varied career as a military adventurer in the fourteenth century (p. 120). The little church stands a little apart on the height; it is a comely little building with its timber spirelet rising above the massive wood baulks typical of Essex belfry-building; it is unique in having a three-storey priests' chamber at the west end; there is an excellent one at Great Wakering near Shoeburyness, but it is of more usual dimensions.

Though very little known, this is one of the great places of England for those who rejoice in mighty views; only Danbury near Colchester in East Anglia has anything to compare with it; there the prospect extends all round a circular horizon but here you look over a more level expanse of less wooded country, and it must compare very strikingly with the wide green sea of the Flanders landscape which can be viewed from Mont Cassel near Dunkirk. It has been warmly praised by Arthur Young, and a century after by Arthur Hissey, most indefatigable of pre-Great-war pony and trap ramblers, as follows: " . . . a glorious expanse of waving woods, green meadows and red-tilled fields; miles of smiling verdure, dotted here and there with scattered farmsteads, red-roofed cottages, with ever and again a peep of a distant church tower or spire. All this goodly prospect, bounded only by the circling blue of the far-away horizon". But the finest feature of all is the broadening Thames estuary from London to the Nore with

Drawn by A. B. Bamford

LAINDON CHURCH, WITH THREE-STOREY PRIESTS' CHAMBER

its peace time slow procession of the shipping of the nations on its way to and from the world's greatest port.

Up the Crouch is the little town of Burnham, to which the crowded masts and white or red sails of its yachts below the close-set red roofs always impart a lively interest. It is eminent for its oyster bed cultivation and as a yachting centre.

All throughout the vast grazing levels that lie between the Crouch and Blackwater estuaries stand solitary the great "halls" or farms among their wide green pastures, subdivided not by hedges but by long dykes full of the vivid green of reeds and bullrushes. Near Sales point opposite Mersea Island is the hamlet of Bradwell-juxta-Mare, of which an interesting Elizabethan map shows the division into cots and crofts of that day. A broad green

98   A QUIET REACH OF THE STOUR NEAR DEDHAM, ESSEX

99   THE STOUR VALLEY AT DEDHAM

track across the fields leads to the sea wall and the site of the Roman fortress of Othona or Ithancester, headquarters of the Count of the Saxon shore, the imperial defence officer against marauding pirates; its vallum and fosse enclose an area of some four acres. It is interesting that this deserted spot was once the chief naval arsenal of Roman Britain, as Portus Rutupiae at Richborough, equally forlorn, was its chief continental trading centre. But the naval centre still functions as a bulwark against the equally obnoxious present-day pirates; it has only shifted a few miles off to the Stour estuary, just as the return of peace will see again the bustle of the ferry port for the European mainland not far from the Roman's haven.

But of even more exciting interest is the gaunt barn, built of stones and tiles from the fort wall, that stands within the enclosure, for this, bereft of east apse and west tower and porch, is almost beyond doubt the torso of the original cathedral of St. Chad, apostle of the Saxon shore. It is known as St. Peter's Chapel, or St. Peter's on the Wall, and may date from the seventh or eighth centuries; here it has stood for some twelve hundred years looking over the flats named after its dedicatory saint to the wide stretches of the grey North Sea,—an outpost of early Christian evangelism superimposed upon a last defensive centre of declining imperial power.

There is no space to do justice to the scattered features of interest between the sea wall and the great Roman East Anglian road; it is a quiet country essentially calling for rambling exploration. There is the little town of Billericay, which came into prominence when two Zeppelins met disaster in the neighbouring district; its name has caused spasms of heart-searchings to generations of etymologists, but we need not follow their discussions, just as there is little need to trench on the controversy regarding the site of the battle of Assandun in 1016, decisive for the Danish conquest of England. Let us glance on our way at the church of West Hanningfield, where the spired and weatherboarded tower is built on the plan of a Greek cross (pp. 7 and 132), and at the comely little brick church of Woodham Walter, with its timber bellcote.

Northward are two churches of typical East country craftsmanship—Great Baddow, practically caught up in Chelmsford suburbs, with fine brick clerestory and octagonal lead spire including a sanctus bell, and Sandon, with a massive diapered brick tower and brick porch; in both of these the corbelling is worked with delicate and sensitive art. It is only a step eastward to Danbury, the Dane-bury where the village stands in the old encampment and its church spire is a landmark for many miles around. If the over optimistic seven hundred feet of some pardonably inexact topographical writers has in the interests of accuracy to be practically halved, its bold ridge commands a view as remarkable for its extent and variety of feature as for its suave grace, though no detailed description can convey its effect, which an actual sight is required to appreciate.

It is a sharp drop and a sharper contrast from Danbury's wooded ridge to Maldon in its marshes (95), though the little town itself is a city set on a hill, and its splendid strategical position on a sharp knoll at the head of an estuary by the confluence of two rivers, the Chelmer and Blackwater or Pant, has made it the scene of desperate struggles. The Anglo-Saxon *Song of Maldon* commemorates the dauntless fight of Ealdorman Byrthnoth against the Vikings, in which he was slain, and Professor Freeman regrets that the classical preoccupations of pedantic pedagogues have left Englishman in ignorance of the heroic trio who kept the bridge,— Wulfstan, Alfbere and Maccus,—in favour of our old friend Horatius. But Maldon is of varied interest in itself as well,—it was Arnold Bennett's ideal estuary town—and its red roofs straggle close set up from the quay side, with the large church of St. Mary's set in trees (95). It is All Saints, however, that is the Parish Church; if its unique triangular tower and spire is its most outstanding feature it has much else of attractive interest. There is probably no connection with the singular triangular tower at Rushton in Northamptonshire, by that mystic Elizabethan recusant Sir Thomas Tresham, preoccupied with the Trinity and the Passion; one can wonder if he had ever heard of his prototype here. If the High Street is modernised there is a plenty of old nooks and curious winding alleys, and we must not forget Dr. Plume's library of 6,000 pre-1760 books, including many fine and precious. They may be seen on application to the vicarage; the ground floor of the red brick home he built for them is the present public library. Unless you are (in peacetime of course) sailing it is best to get to Mersea and Brightlingsea through the villages, taking on the way Layer Marney Hall, where the eight-storeyed twin gate-towers of Tudor brick and terra-cotta surpass in height at least the earlier efforts at Hadleigh deanery and Oxburgh Hall in the northern East Anglian counties. The church has a fine brick arcade, and the tomb of one Lord Marney is carried out in the same delicate Renaissance terra-cotta as the detail of the Hall. To Colchester not even a cursory ramble can be devoted though it is well worth while to explore Holy Trinity's Saxon tower, the vast castle, now Museum, largely built of Roman tile-bricks, St. John's Abbey Gateway, the fine Georgian *Red Lion* Inn, the *Marquis of Granby's* Tudor interior and John Belcher's big Baroque town hall on the height. We must press on to Mersea Island, the reverse of flat, with the tower of one of its two churches peeping out of the trees seen across the shining water of the narrow strait, and the little yachting and oyster centre of Brightlingsea, where the tall church tower is a prominent landmark and 185 tiles in the church commemorate as many natives drowned all over the seven seas. Further up the estuary is Wivenhoe, a townlet of fishermen, boat-builders, and a great place for supplying boat crews. But what has become of the long house covered with a masterpiece of pargetted plaster patterns (p. 48), on which the Historical Monuments Commission reported as "condition—poor"?

St. Osyth makes a pleasant picture from the creek as its old red roofed houses straggle up to the red brick church tower which accords with the fine brick arcades, in the interior. Of the Priory much remains incorporated in a private mansion; it is entered through an impressive twin-bayed gateway in panelled flint which parallels St. John's we noticed at Colchester. The legendary story of St. Osyth is well known; it may be actual fact that she was beheaded by the Danes, but when the late fifteenth century Abbey buildings took shape the institution had long ceased to be a nunnery. St. Osyth was a favourite saint of the middle ages; it was customary to make a + in the ashes and pray to "St. Sith" against harm. We are now in the Tendring Hundred, where the suffix le-Soken to the hamlet names of Thorpe and Kirby recalls Danish overlordship. The trio of Clacton, Frinton, and Walton may be gladly left to the eulogies of the publicity folders, and not till this tyranny be overpast can the old town of Harwich be readily visited, or the modern adjunct of Parkstone take up the threads of its sea traffic to Antwerp and Holland. But Manningtree at the head of the estuary is full of nooks and corners above its wide sweeping marshes, and Mistley, long its mother parish, has the scanty remains of a grandiose scheme for an elaborate eighteenth century bathing establishment devised by a contemporary plutocrat, who commissioned no less a person than the celebrated architect Robert Adam. The scheme did not get very far, but Adam rebuilt the church in his own style as a wide hall between two tandem cupola-capped steeples in diminishing stages. A wealthy vicar in 1870 demolished the church in favour of a "neat edifice in the Early Decorated style" on another site nearer the station. But the towers remain, separate and forlorn (with the one serving as a mausoleum) it is said with the approval of the Admiralty, who find them excellent as landmarks.

Above Manningtree the wide marshy Stour estuary (97) contracts suddenly to the quiet scale of Constable's river (98); its peaceful charm, its unpretending yet gracious variety remain happily unchanged since his day, and if one writer on country England fled to an intensely rural spot in Suffolk because his hamlet here had an access of week-end dwellers, he may perhaps be not unfairly regarded as hyper-sensitive. From the Essex side we look across to the gentle winding wooded slopes opposite which neighbour Suffolk shares with our county; we shall not grudge them their part in this exquisitely typical stretch of England recorded for the world by the genius of her greatest painter. And we shall not repine that most of the noble and famous places by the Stour lie across the border; we have the delightfulness of

Dedham, whose tower and district (99) he loved as well and painted as often as any. Constable left his impression in well-chosen words as well as in inimitable colour: "The beauty of the surrounding scenery, its gentle declivities, its luxuriant meadow flats sprinkled with flocks and herds, its well-cultivated uplands, its woods and rivers with numerous scattered villages and churches, farms and picturesque cottages, all impart to this particular spot an elegance hardly anywhere else to be found,—nothing can exceed the beautiful appearance of the country, its freshness, its amenity". With this we can take our farewell of the Home Counties, for Constable has here set down for all time the character of this Essex, of these Home Counties, nay of loved and lovely England herself,—the countryside which it is our privilege to defend against the gates of hell infernal itself, and which by the mercy of God and the striving of her sons and daughters shall be handed down unspoilt and unravaged to the generations who shall come after.

Drawn by J. Charles Wall

THE BELFRY TIMBERING, WEST HANNINGFIELD

INDEX

The figures in *heavy type* give references to the *figure numbers* of the photographic illustrations; f prefixed to a page number denotes a reference to a line drawing on that page.

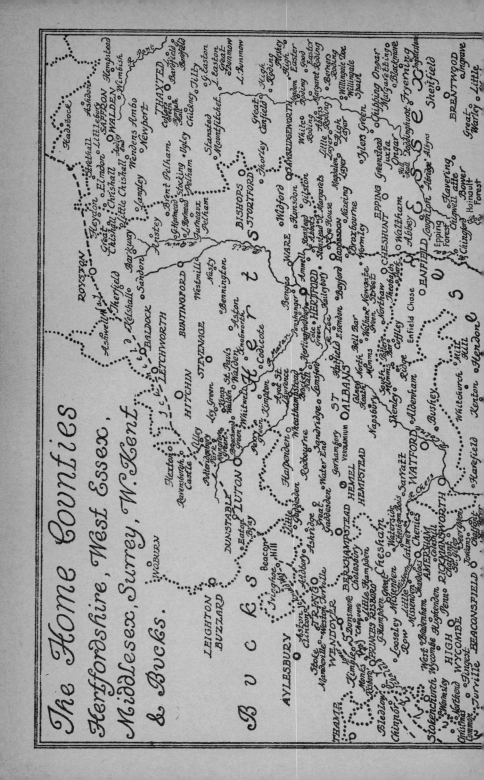

The Home Counties
Hertfordshire, West Essex,
Middlesex, Surrey, W. Kent
& Bucks.